YOUR CALLING

GORDON T. SMITH

HERE
AND
NOW

MAKING SENSE
OF VOCATION

ivp

An imprint of InterVarsity Press
Downers Grove, Illinois

InterVarsity Press
P.O. Box 1400 | Downers Grove, IL 60515-1426
ivpress.com | email@ivpress.com

InterVarsity Press® is the publishing division of InterVarsity Christian Fellowship/USA®. For more information, visit intervarsity.org.

Scripture quotations, unless otherwise noted, are from the New Revised Standard Version Bible, copyright © 1989 National Council of the Churches of Christ in the United States of America. Used by permission. All rights reserved worldwide.

While any stories in this book are true, some names and identifying information may have been changed to protect the privacy of individuals.

The publisher cannot verify the accuracy or functionality of website URLs used in this book beyond the date of publication.

Cover design and image composite: David Fassett
Interior design: Daniel van Loon
Images: two hands: © CSA Images / Getty Images
        paper texture: from True Grit Paper Supply

ISBN 978-1-5140-0341-1 (print) | ISBN 978-1-5140-0342-8 (digital)

Printed in the United States of America ♾

Library of Congress Cataloging-in-Publication Data
Names: Smith, Gordon T., 1953- author.
Title: Your calling here and now : making sense of vocation / Gordon T.
    Smith.
Description: Downers Grove, IL : InterVarsity Press, [2022] | Includes
    bibliographical references.
Identifiers: LCCN 2022004083 (print) | LCCN 2022004084 (ebook) | ISBN
    9781514003411 (print) | ISBN 9781514003428 (digital)
Subjects: LCSH: Vocation–Christianity.
Classification: LCC BV4740 .S635 2022 (print) | LCC BV4740 (ebook) | DDC
    253.5–dc23/eng/20220223
LC record available at https://lccn.loc.gov/2022004083
LC ebook record available at https://lccn.loc.gov/2022004084

26   25   24   23   22 | 6   5   4   3   2   1

for joella

ALSO AVAILABLE FROM GORDON T. SMITH

CONTENTS

PREFACE

WE LIVE OUR LIVES by intentional response to the calling and initiative of God. We do not live self-constructed lives; rather, the meaning of our existence is that we live open to and attentive to what we sense God is saying to us. It follows that it is appropriate for us to then ask what it means for each of us to be stewards of the one unique and remarkable life that has been given to us. What does it mean to do what we have been invited by the Creator to do? What does it mean to respond to the invitation of God to participate in what God is doing as Creator and redeemer of the world? What does it mean for each of us, within the particulars of our circumstances, to live out the call to love our neighbor as God has in Christ loved us? And in all of this, what does it mean for us to see our daily lives, our chores, our engagement with the world as having sacred significance—not just specific religious activities, but each action, each word spoken, each way of being present to our world?

In reflecting on the significance of our lives and our work, I am indebted to the sixteenth century Reformers. On the one hand, we recognize that Protestant Reformers John Calvin and Martin Luther fundamentally altered the conversation about vocation when they opened up our vision of life and work to an appreciation of how each Christian was called, and that God was and is calling women and men into all walks of life and work. On the other, we cannot miss the remarkable contribution of Catholic reformer Ignatius Loyola, with his affirmation that God speaks to and is present to each person, in love, and each person has the capacity to know the *particular* calling and grace of God.

Taken together, we have a powerful affirmation of the significance of each human life, lived out in the world in response to God's call. Further, we can then consider what this means for each one of us to think about our lives, our work, and our vocations. What follows—this question, the meaning of our lives and our work in the here and now—will be considered from different perspectives. The opening two chapters speak of vocation as something found at the intersection of this person, at this time, and in this place. These two chapters are foundational as they set the stage for what follows.

The next two chapters speak of the tensions we often feel when it comes to vocation as we wrestle with multiple vocations—the varied ways in which we are called to be present to our world. In these chapters, we will consider the need to face transitions with grace and courage.

Then I move to two chapters where I speak to thoughtfulness and to the work of our hands. Initially, I invite the reader to value and affirm the life of the mind as essential to our capacity to fulfill our vocations. And, as the complement, a chapter on the work of our hands and the calling to crafts and trades. I suggest to the reader that both of these—our minds and our hands—are an essential complement to our lives and our work, regardless of our callings.

Another chapter follows that speaks of the intersection of our personal vocations with the organizations in which those callings are located. From there, I speak to what I will call "practices of engagement"—spiritual practices that foster our capacity to be attentive to where and how God is present and acting in our world. Finally, I speak to hope: the virtue and disposition without which we cannot live—the resilient hopefulness that necessarily must undergird our lives and our work.

Each chapter has a simple agenda: to foster our capacity to make sense of our lives, our work, and very specifically, the calling of God. But also, I would like to encourage good conversation about our lives and our work. I will frequently stress that while we need to take personal responsibility for our lives, we need the company of others to help us make sense of the particulars of our situation and the challenges we personally face or feel. To this end, consider reading this guide to vocation along with another—a friend or spouse, a study group, or perhaps a group of friends on the journey— reflecting together on the questions posed at the end of each chapter.

T THIS TIME AND
N THIS PLACE

VOCATION IS ALWAYS PARTICULAR: this person, at this time, and in this place.[1] Vocation is never discerned in a historical vacuum; it is always in the specifics of the world in which we live. It is always about the *here and now*—and, as needs to be stressed, it is the here and now as it comes to us, as it presents itself, not as we wish it to be. We get beyond wishful thinking, and we name reality and discern calling in the light of and in the midst of this time and this place—*this* situation.

Therefore, we ask, at this time and in this place, who and what are we called to be and do? What does it mean to steward our lives in light of our economic circumstances, marital status and family situation, age, and personal health? What does it mean to be attentive to what we bring to the table in a way that takes full account of our social and cultural context, as well as the economic and political situation in which we are living, locally and globally?

WE ASK, AT THIS TIME AND IN THIS PLACE, WHO AND WHAT ARE WE CALLED TO BE AND DO? Vocation and calling are about much more than our occupation or job or career. It certainly includes the work for which we are responsible—whether waged or volunteer or managing a home with the whole range of domestic activities so vital to what it means to call a place "home." But it also includes the network of social and family connections that are an essential part of our lives. And so, within the midst of all we are and all we are responsible for and those we are responsible to, we ask the question, What am I being called to say and do?

This applies to us both individually and collectively. An organization or business or development agency or school is always needing to ask, What are we called to be and do now, at this time and in this place? A college or university will ask what it means to be invested in higher education in this season of the life of a country or city or community—in this time and in this place. A church—collectively—will ask what it means to be this faith community at this time and in this location—this neighborhood, this chapter in the history of this community and, in the intersection of this time and this place, to be this church. We do not have the luxury of imagining another set of circumstances: it is always at this time and in this place that we make sense of the identity and mission of the organizations of which we are a part.

While this principle applies to both organizations and individuals, the focus here will be more on the individual. This is not to discount the shared responsibilities we have. It is merely a matter of focus and the need to not lose the grace and power of the individual in the matrix of time and space and within the confluence and complexities of our organizations and collective concerns. What comes here is an appeal: for each person to ask of themselves, In this time and in this place, how am I being called to speak and act? To be more specific, this is a call to name our situation on the assumption that calling is always—always—for this time and for this place. It is always a calling to and in this particular set of circumstances.

Sometimes the circumstances we face are thrust upon us. Those of us who serve in higher education in North America will for many years remember the weekend of March 13-14, 2020. Everything changed—and dramatically so—when we realized the coronavirus pandemic meant, quite simply, it would not be business as usual. We needed to make a call: In this time and in this place, what does it mean for us to do what needs to be done? No more, but most assuredly no less. For many of us, we were taken by surprise. Perhaps we should have seen this coming, having watched the outbreak in China and northern Italy. Perhaps, indeed, we should have had a contingency plan in place. But as it happened, the decision had to be made very quickly to move to an alternate form of fulfilling our mission as a university. And in the process, many organizations, churches, and agencies were using the same word—it was heard again and again— "pivot." We shifted, adapted, responded, and did all we could to sustain our work and mission in response to dramatically changing circumstances.

More often than not, the recognition of vocation typically emerges more slowly, over time. As we come to a gradual realization of the particulars of our lives and of our situations, we begin to process what this means and how we are necessarily being called to read these situations as we come to clarity about what it is we are being called to do: in this time and in this place.

NO MORE AND NO LESS

The genius of getting this right is appreciating not only this intersection—of this person at this time and in this place— but very specifically accepting and embracing this situation and our role or calling within it. Clarity of vocation means knowing what we do but also what we do not need to do. We accept that some things will not be our focus or our responsibility. But more, it is also about what we say—where and how we speak—as well as what we leave unsaid. To say what needs to be said and to say no more. No less, certainly, but no more. To know when it is best that a thought or impression or conviction is left unsaid. And, further, to know what needs to be done—at this time and in this place—and what can and must be left undone. We do not need to live with any compulsion to speak or act beyond what is called for in the particulars of this time and place. Wise women and men do not over-speak, but rather say what needs to be said with courage and grace, doing what is essential and needful. We do not live frenetically trying to be and do as much as possible, but rather have a sense of time and place, what we need to be and do, together with a peace and settledness of heart regarding what is not needful.

4

In part, this is true because there is growth beyond the felt need to be a hero, to be constantly fixing things, or to be affirmed for all we have done or accomplished or contributed. We are content to do no more than what it is we have been called to do. This includes that which is done in obscurity—where the work we do is simply done because it needs to be done, whether or not we are thanked or affirmed for it.

> **CLARITY OF VOCATION MEANS KNOWING WHAT WE DO BUT ALSO WHAT WE DO NOT NEED TO DO.**

Whether as president of the United States or the homemaker who knows the laundry needs to be done today, in each vocation, we live in the grace of doing what needs to be done. No more and no less.

This means we do what we have been called to do. In so doing, we realize many people are involved in running an organization and that within the whole—this organization, this church, this agency—we need clarity about the specifics of what we are called to contribute. And so, we can ask: What, within the economy of lives and responsibilities, is necessary on my to-do list? Vocation is about doing what is needful, what falls to us to do as our work and sphere of responsibility. It is either myself or a sibling who will care for my mother in her senior years. Either I do the laundry, or it does not get done. As president of this college, I cannot deflect or demur or equivocate; I need to do what this organization needs from the president. Either the president does it or it does not get done. As pastor of this congregation, as manager of this department store, I need to do what I need to do.

When we speak about this time and this place, it also means we have come to accept what some speak of as the poverty of time. Many seem to live with the constant battle of wishing they had more time, routinely missing deadlines on assignments or responsibilities, having to apologize for delays in this or that or the other. Yes, of course, there will be times in our lives when we feel the impossibility of it all and wish time would do us just a simple favor and stand still so we could catch up. There is a health crisis in the family at the time a major business negotiation is on the table—so we make a quick trip to drop in on an aging parent, confirm they are okay, and we are back to the office working late to finalize the terms of the deal, grateful we did not get caught in a major traffic jam in our comings and goings. Or we are running late for a flight, not because of bad planning or foresight, but merely because something came up with our teenager that meant we were not going to leave the house without first being present to this young person and their concern or "crisis"—and yes, I put crisis in quotations fully recognizing that what this teen is going to wear that day may not qualify as a crisis(!) against the possibility that you would miss your flight. But you know *this* matters more right now, and so in the end you are caught in the security line wondering why the agent needs to take so long to check each ID.

But those times can and must be the exception. In the normal flow of our lives, vocational thinking and acting means there is a *leisured* pace to our lives. We are not constantly at war against the limits of hours, trying to be more and to accomplish more than we are called to be and do. We learn what it means to live in the fullness of time, with time as friend, and grace-filled space for life and work and relationships rather than always complaining time is not on our side.

If two assignments are due at the same time, we learn to do today what needs to be done today so the deadline down the road is met. A young person might be living in the moment and only tackle an assignment on the day prior to when it is due, thus facing a personal crisis when they suddenly realize they have two assignments due on the same day. But as we mature and learn to live in time, we see what is on the horizon and do today what needs to be done today so that we are ready for tomorrow.

I will grant that thinking this way is a luxury. For the majority of humans, they have thrust upon them tasks and responsibilities about which they have no choice. They are in survival mode. But for those who can step back and reflect—for most of those who will have a copy of this book in their hands—we can approach this question by asking what it means to be good stewards of our time and place in the flow of history and the circumstances of our lives. Do not underestimate your options here; even if your life circumstances seem all consuming, do read with a thought to where there might be the option for attending to the margins of your life that might open up space for doing something that matters to you.

BEYOND WISHFUL THINKING AND REGRETS

When we speak about the here and now, we do so with a frank and honest read of our time and our situation. We face our reality. There is no effective capacity to discern and embrace vocation unless and until we name our reality; vocation is always—always—about the here and now. In *this* time, in *this* place.

It is so very easy to say "if only"—if only this or that or the other had not occurred. If only this had not happened to us as a child or in our teen years. If only we had not been fired from our job. If only this illness or accident had not come our way. But the problem is that in so doing, we live looking back rather than facing and living within our current reality and accepting that this is now our new reality. And it makes no difference if what has happened is a result of our own doing: we mishandled our job or a relationship or very simply did something inappropriate and now are living with the consequences. Or, if the situation we are facing is due to something another person did—however wrong it was or continues to be. In both instances, one is a victim, either of one's own foolishness or the misdeeds of others. And yet, regardless of the original cause, this is now our reality. Discerning vocation is a matter of getting beyond the "if only," which leads to wasted emotional and intellectual energy.

> THERE IS NO EFFECTIVE CAPACITY TO DISCERN AND EMBRACE VOCATION UNLESS AND UNTIL WE NAME OUR REALITY.

We also learn to get beyond nostalgia—the propensity to look back fondly or wistfully to an earlier time. We turn from longing for a previous time and ask about the *here and now*: this time, this place. This is not a matter of fatalistic resignation; rather, we do this in hope. We ask, What can and must be done now in light of what is *actually* the case rather than what we wish was the case? This is not because we are only living for today; it is merely that today is all we have and so, looking to today and down the road, we choose where and how we will act. Here and now.

And in this, it is important to remember we cannot map out the rest of our lives. We choose and discern in light of today, and we know the rest of our lives will be lived out one day at a time, one step at a time. We are merely affirming and embracing what we are called to do today—with hope and grace and courage.

When I became a university president, I came into a situation where the institution was carrying an inordinate amount of debt. And sure, once or twice I bemoaned the situation and wondered what factors might have led to this challenging situation. In other words, there might be a space for a little raging and ranting, if you must. Perhaps go out to a quiet spot on the beach and yell and scream. Fine. But then, turn, and rather than say "if only," consider what must be said and what must be done in light of what is *actually* the case rather than what we wish was the case. In my case, it meant that as the president, it was my job to help the institution move to a stronger level of financial sustainability. And I needed to do this while keeping the university on mission. Sure, it was not what I would have chosen, but that is not the point. This was the situation that presented itself, and this was the situation in which I had been called to speak and to act.

Sometimes, this is a particularly difficult pill to swallow. The way before us is closed. Our position is terminated. We were denied admission to a college or university. The publisher turned down our book proposal. We feel the sting of this setback. But now we are asking, in light of not what we wish was the case but what is actually the case: How do we choose to act and move forward, one step at a time?

TENDING TO WHAT MATTERS

The here and now is also about tending to what *matters*—what is essential, pivotal, and crucial to this place and this time. To use the language of Jesus in his encounter with Martha, speaking about her sister Mary (Luke 10:38-42), we ask of ourselves: What is the one thing needful? What do I need to tend to today? What do I need to say? And what can be left unsaid? What do I need to do? And what can be left for another day? There may be an imperative as simple and uncomplicated as, this is recycling day on our street, so I need to set out the bins for the trucks that come through to collect our discarded bottles. Or it may be that there is a board meeting on the horizon, and so today I need to be doing the first draft of my report to the board. Or, if you are a gardener, if you are going to harvest in the fall, you need to plant in the spring. If we are going to travel on such and such a date, then we need to book our flights today.

We are always tending to both: what needs to be done this day, today; and what needs to be tended to now, today, because the deadline or due date is on the horizon. I intentionally mention recycling day to highlight there is both the work of chairing an important board meeting or being ready for a speaking engagement as well as the ordinary, the mundane, the routine of domestic duties that are simply part of what it means to be human. We tend to both.

But then, when we speak of what matters, we recognize this is not always a simple question. As we all know, it can be quite complicated because life is so frequently filled with uncertainty and ambiguity. As such, it is helpful to think in terms of what we might appropriately speak of as *principled pragmatism*. We live constantly in the dynamic of the here and now where we name our reality, face the circumstances, and get beyond regret and nostalgia; but just as assuredly, we are attentive to what *can* happen and how our ideals, our hopes and aspirations, our principles *can* inform a situation.

If we are in a leadership role within a business or an organization or civic agency or church, we likely have a conviction about what this organization should be like and what it should be doing and what should be happening. We live with this vision or ideal as a constant in our minds. We would not be in leadership if this were not the case: that as individuals of deep-felt conviction and principle, we have a vision for what it means to be the church as a pastor, or to be a university if we are in leadership within academia, or in politics if we are seeking to foster legislation leading to good and fruitful outcomes. But we also live with and work with significant limitations: financial, political, and circumstantial.

In our personal lives, we do this all the time. We think, *This is what an ideal house would look like for us.* And we also recognize, *However, this is what we can afford—this house is close to work or school or church.* That is, we are not purists or idealists or mere dreamers. We know how to live and work within the limitations of our actual circumstances.

11

Acting in the here and now, though, also means we live by the principle of *gradual incrementalism*: the perspective that we can take small steps, incremental steps, that move us toward a long-term vision or ideal outcome. We do today what needs to be done today to move us to where we need to be tomorrow. Sometimes this is a building project or an art project that is completed one small step at a time. But then also, this requires a long-term vision imbued with patience in that we are taking small steps in the face of unjust systems, or a less than ideal organizational culture or society, or a major project.

And yet the bottom line remains: in the here and now, in these life circumstances, we ask what we need to be saying and doing. What needs to be done just because it needs to be done? And more, in what ways, and specifically through what *incremental* steps, can we, with principled pragmatism, move our organizations and our living situation and our relationships, at home and at work, one step at a time in the direction we need to be going?

FOUR ESSENTIAL CAPACITIES

Living well and working well, in the here and now, in this time and in this place—coming to the present where we do and say no more and no less than we are called to do and say—means we are fully present and able to discern our calling. Doing this requires, at the very least, four indispensable capacities: focus, courage, connectedness, and patience.

Focus is a challenge in that we are seeking to make sense of calling in the midst of what has aptly been called an age of distraction. We are so easily and thus so constantly interrupted by this or that expectation or demand—the assumption that we are always "on" and always available to respond to a text or email message as our devices prompt us to tend to whoever or whatever is calling for our attention. In what follows, the assumption all along will be that discerning vocation, by its very nature, is a slow and deliberative process. We come to clarity out of a focused reflection represented, perhaps, by the leisured walk on the beach— alone, with no device in hand—such that head and heart are moving at the pace we are walking.

Focus also means we come to terms with the myriad expectations others have of us—whether within our family system, within our religious subculture, or within the organizations where we work or serve as volunteers. The expectations of others should not be dismissed; they may well be legitimate in that some expectations are the rightful requirements of what it means to be married or what it means to have a job that includes doing and accomplishing certain things. Or we signed up for a course and the professor understandably expects a level of engagement in the class activities and the assignments outlined in the syllabus. We do not disregard legitimate expectations. But that is why focus is so very important: that with it, we are able to set aside those expectations that are a weight rather than a genuine form of accountability. In this regard, we can always assume there will inevitably be those who are not happy with us or our work. Vocational thinking and acting are not about being popular; it is about saying what needs to be said and doing what needs doing. Yes, we need to be accountable, but we will always have those who do not affirm us. And for this, we need *focus*—a settled heart and mind.

Focus also means we set aside the immediately gratifying, that which brings a quick emotional high—the immediate thanks or affirmation or recognition or even, literally, the quick payback in terms of cash in hand. Focus means deferred gratification and, as we need to stress again and again, the capacity to work in obscurity—quietly and persistently doing what needs to be done, far from the distracting gaze of others, with either their critique or their affirmation or adulation.

In an age of distraction, we are only present to the here and now if we grow in our capacity for focus.

Ask yourself what you can do to foster this capacity for focus—for seeing and feeling the here and the now with clarity. For some of us, it comes through the extended walk—perhaps as a daily exercise or routine: alone, without a cell phone, without interruption, to walk a country road long enough to come to a measured appreciation of the particulars of your situation. Slowly, at the rate of a steady

> IN AN AGE OF DISTRACTION, WE ARE ONLY PRESENT TO THE HERE AND NOW IF WE GROW IN OUR CAPACITY FOR FOCUS.

and purposeful pace, to gain a purchase on one's own thoughts and feelings and be able to weigh alternatives.

Second, we also ask for *courage* in what has aptly been called an age of anxiety. When such a high percentage of those we live and work with are caught up in a cycle of fretfulness and worry, the grace we seek is the simple but compelling courage to not only see what needs to be said and done but then also the will to do it—the courage to say the uncomfortable word, the difficult word, and the courage to do what needs to be done. We not only recognize what is required; we *act*. Crucial here, though, is that we recognize the courage needed to keep silent when a word is not appropriate or necessary. And also, it means we can be at peace to let something be, to let it go, because whatever it is, it is either the right time or the right place or not ultimately our responsibility. We have peace—read *courage*—to not act, for whatever reason, when there might be pressure or expectation or some compulsion to act.

And courage is, of course, the antithesis to fear. Those who choose well—vocationally—are not so much those who have no fears as rather those who actually recognize their fears and anxieties and have learned what it means, even in the face of those fears, to do what needs to be done. They have that level of self-awareness and as such the capacity to act even in the midst of the swirl of anxiety that is all around them.

Third, those who choose well—in this time and in this place—are, inevitably, *connected* with significant friends and co-discerners. We live in what might be called—for the sake of parallel with the age of distraction and the age of anxiety—an age of disconnection. So many live staggeringly lonely lives. They do not have the capacity or opportunity (or both) for grace-filled conversation with another where, with freedom and without fear, they can speak about themselves and their lives and their choices and challenges.

The point that needs to be made over and over is that no one else can discern your vocation for you. It is for you to go alone to your "garden of Gethsemane," for you to have your own meeting with the angel Gabriel, for you to have your own burning bush encounter with the one who beckons you to be what you are being called to be.[2] No one can do this for you. But you cannot do it if you are only alone. We make sense of what it means to know and hear God when we are alone; we each must learn the grace of solitude. But solitude—the lonely extended walk, perhaps—only brings clarity and the courage to act if we are in community, if we are connected. On the one hand this is so because all of our choices and actions involve others—spouse, friends, and colleagues. We need to be genuinely responsive to the needs and expectations of others. We do not live in our personal bubble. We need to ask, What does spouse, child, parent, colleague, neighbor—my country, my church, my workplace—need from me? Yes, we can and must speak about misguided generosity, where our whole lives are lived responsive to the needs of others—when we are not suffi-ciently attentive to what we are called to do. But we are in community; we do live interconnectedly with the needs— the genuine needs—of others.

Further, we need community and connectedness as well because we each have a remarkable capacity for self-deception. We cannot simply presume that every impression, every longing, ambition, or aspiration is from God. Our longings, fears, and inclinations need the check and confir-mation that comes from gracious and frank conversations with those who know us well, will not flatter us, will speak truth to us, and will call us to account for the ways in which either a misguided ambition will lead us pell-mell over a cliff, or provide reassurance when our fears and anxieties keep us from doing what we need to do. We need those in our lives who can simply say "no, that is not you; let that dream go," and who can also nudge us to do what our fear of failure is keeping us from embracing. But more, we need encouragement. We need conversations with those who will affirm but not flatter us, who will challenge us when preconceived notions or presumed agendas are blinding us about something we should perhaps be doing or saying. We need those in our lives who will say the words we need to hear, such as "you are a poet," "you need to write," "you can and should perhaps go back to school," or whatever it might be they say to us that we need to hear so we can embrace this time and this place.

And then, fourth, we need patience. In a time and culture where patience is almost viewed as a weakness, we urgently need to recover the ancient spiritual wisdom that patience is a virtue and that we can only be truly present in this time and this place if we are patient, able to wait, able to let things unfold in a timely manner. In a social environment consumed by haste, we embrace a leisured approach to life and work, seeking to do what is timely rather than being consumed with frenetic busyness. We will learn the grace of patience: we will have the courage to do now what needs to be done and the courage to know when to wait and let other things— however important—happen in due time.

What all of this speaks to is that we do not live on autopilot, and we are not only driven or determined by our circumstances. We choose and we act. We recognize that in this time and in this place, we need to be intentional in

taking the time for solitude, for attention to our circumstances, for time and space to name our fears and anxieties,
and for intentional conversation with those who come
alongside as we discern vocational questions—questions
about how we live out the call of God on our lives, in the
here and now.

QUESTIONS FOR REFLECTION AND DISCUSSION

1. What is your situation, your "at this time and in this
   place"? As you read this chapter, what came to mind about
   the particulars of your circumstances? What does it mean
   for you to name your reality?

2. In your situation, what is imperative—it simply has to
   be done?

3. What is your greatest need in order for you to be present
   in the here and now? Focus? Courage? Connectedness
   with others? Patience?

THE STEWARDSHIP
OF OUR LIVES

THE JUDEO-CHRISTIAN RELIGIOUS HERITAGE affirms the incomparable worth of each individual person—created in the image of God and a means by which, in word and deed, the reign of God is fulfilled in the world. We can and must affirm the significance and the potential of each person, before God and as a participant in the purposes of God in creation—in the healing and redemption of the created order. Each person is created out of God's deep intentionality; no one is an accident. No one. Each person is born into a world where the first and fundamental thing about them is that they are chosen by and loved by God.

Yes, we insist that an individual is never purely an isolated spiritual monad—that a

TO BE A PERSON IS TO BE CONNECTED.

genuine understanding of the individual locates a person, an individual self, within a village, a society, a community. To be a person is to be connected. And yet, saying this in no way diminishes the beauty and significance of the individual person in his or her own right. We reject radical individualism—the individual disconnected from community. And we also decry self-centered narcissism. But then, with these caveats, we can and do affirm the inherent worth and significance of each person and thus the value and potential of each person's work.

THE WORTH AND SIGNIFICANCE OF OUR WORK

In affirming the significance of each person, it also follows that we take note of what each person does—their work. We appreciate the value and worth of each person's contributions. This further means that we recognize the significance and meaning of *human agency*—that is, that words and deeds, what we say and what we do, make a difference. We can, without doubt, overstate the significance of our actions and words. But when this overestimation happens, we do not need the overcorrection that dismisses or discounts our words and our actions. Rather, we can and must locate human agency within and as part of the purposes and actions of God in the world. We do not need to assume that in speaking of God as God and the preeminence of the glory of God, that we would completely discount the contributions that persons can and should make, and that we shouldn't recognize the significance of these actions. That is, we can stress that God is God and the author of all things. But that does not mean we then insist human actions are of little, if any, value, or that human endeavor in the end amounts to little, if anything. We do not need to discount or dismiss the work and contribution of each person as a way by which we preserve the conviction we must have that all is of God and is offered back to God. We can affirm the unique glory, power, and beauty of God and, with grace and humility, speak to how each person is not only of incomparable worth, but also what we say and what we do actually make a difference. We are agents, not merely observers; we are players in the drama of God's creative and redemptive purposes.

In the narrative that describes the exodus out of Egypt and into the Promised Land, there is no doubt for the reader that this is God's work. God is redeeming his people and leading them out of slavery. But the story only makes sense when we see the extraordinary role human players had in making it happen. God calls Moses, and then Moses is a critical factor in whether or not the people of Israel make it to the Promised Land. Similarly, the angel Gabriel comes to Mary and invites her to accept the work of the Spirit, and we are taken by her humble response: "Here am I, the servant of the Lord; let it be with me according to your word" (Lk 1:38). Further, it was not an arbitrary calling wherein Saul, who became the apostle Paul, was selected to bring the gospel to the Gentile world. He himself is fully aware of this, having all of the credentials of a Jewish Rabbi coupled with his citizenship in Rome, which he leverages without hesitation. It is no surprise we see the call to young Timothy—a call from Paul himself at the conclusion of his career—that he, Timothy, must cultivate and steward the gift of God that was given to him: that is, to be all that he, Timothy, had been called to be (2 Tim 1:6-7).

Back to the apostle Paul. When he thinks of his own calling and that of his colleagues and peers, he speaks of how he and his readers are ambassadors and, even more amazing, that they are *coworkers* with God (2 Cor 6:1). On the one hand, we do not overstate what this means: no, they and we are not peers with God in the work of God. But what we can affirm is that we are not mere pawns in the chessboard of history. Thus, the psalmist prays and has no problem asking "us":

> May God be gracious to us and bless us
> and make his face to shine upon us. (Ps 67:1)

This blessing is to the end that the name of God would be revered to the ends of the earth (Ps 67:1), but the means to that end is an affirmation of the blessing of the psalmist on "us." Or consider Psalm 90 and the prayer that the work of our hands would prosper (Ps 90:17)—that our work would be marked by weight and significance and continuing worth in the eyes of God. This longing for meaningful work that makes a difference is, then, something that has been placed in our hearts by the Creator.

God always remains the central and defining character in the drama. We would not wish it otherwise. All things are from God and are done to the glory of God. But with that baseline and vision of God and the world, we can and necessarily *need* to speak—with humility, but also with confidence—of the human vocation and calling: to see and appreciate that vocation is found at the intersection of *this* person with this time and this place.

VOCATION IS FOUND AT THE INTERSECTION OF *THIS* PERSON WITH THIS TIME AND THIS PLACE.

We *can* celebrate the work of a business entrepreneur. We *can* appreciate the mastery of a fifth-grade schoolteacher. We *can* affirm the valuable contribution an organizational leader brings through skill and persistence so her department flourishes and the whole organization is on mission. We *can* revel in the power and glory and beauty of the work of a musician—be they composer or performer. That is, we celebrate talent and ability and skill, and we appreciate that diligence in our work leads to outcomes where it is entirely appropriate to say, *You* did it! *You* made it happen. You leveraged your skill, you invested the time, you persisted through difficulty and set back, and now *you* have done it. *You* preached a superb sermon. *You* published a book that will be invaluable for your readership. *You* built up a restaurant business and it is a thriving success. *You* are clearly a master gardener and the space you have designed and cultivated is a place of beauty and serenity, alive with plant life and birdsong. And to one and all, we say, "Thank you." It is *their* work. It is *their* contribution and *their* offering. We celebrate their accomplishments. We commend them. We thank them. We pray that God would establish the work of their hands as in Psalm 90. Again, saying this in no way takes away from the glory of God; God is not in any way diminished by our celebration of the work and contribution and excellence offered by this person in this time and in this place.

This is why we use the language of *stewardship* to highlight that there is no such thing as a generic person, a pawn in the hands of the divine chess player. We ask: What does it mean to steward this life, the life of *this* person? And then further, we can ask: What does it mean to be accountable for the quality and character of our work? We speak of account-ability very specifically *because* our work matters; what we say and what we do make a difference. And so, we rightly disdain mediocrity and the shoddy exercise of a trade or a craft or a speaker or lecturer who is clearly just winging it. We are accountable, and we call one another to do our best, to bring our skills to the fore, and to steward our time so that we can do what needs to be done and do it with excellence.

KNOWING OURSELVES IN TRUTH

When we speak of the significance of the human individual—the inherent worth and the capacity of each person, before God, to be a player in the drama and purposes of God—we also recognize and affirm the *uniqueness* of each person. Each person is a distinct and unrepeatable representation of the image of God in the world. Even identical twins know this; they are different, and as such they have their own in-dividual identity. Therefore, when we speak of vocation as the intersection of this person with this time and this place, it is not just any person, but *this* person of which we speak. And this may be an awkward way to put it, but no one knows this person quite like this person. Without doubt, mothers will have an intimate knowledge of each of their children, and spouses who have been married over multiple decades know each other rather well. But in the end, there is no sub-stitute for *self*-knowledge. It may well be that the greatest obstacle to being fully present to the here and now is the failure to know oneself: the inability to see oneself truth-fully. We need to long for and seek this self-awareness: no illusions, no lies, no pretention or facades. To see oneself in truth and come to the grace of living faithfully and humbly within one's own skin.

On the one hand, this means we stop wishing we were or are anyone other than who we are. We might well wish our lives had unfolded differently, perhaps even wishing we had been born into a different family, or a different social network, or a different country, or a different time. But if we are going to live and work with vocational integrity, at some point we come to a gracious acceptance of who we are, and leverage what it is we bring to the table, to the drama, to the work required in this time and in this place.

THE GREATEST OBSTACLE TO BEING FULLY PRESENT TO THE HERE AND NOW IS THE FAILURE TO KNOW ONESELF: THE INABILITY TO SEE ONESELF TRUTHFULLY.

Along the way, we grow in self-knowledge and learn to speak truthfully to ourselves. In one of the most quoted lines in Dostoevsky's *The Brothers Karamazov*, the elder Zosima is speaking to the father of the three Karamazov brothers, and he insists: "Above all, do not lie to yourself. A man who lies to himself and listens to his own lie comes to a point where he does not discern any truth either in himself or anywhere around him, and thus falls into disrespect towards himself and others."[1] The poignancy of this declaration from elder Zosima is that as Dostoevsky's magisterial novel unfolds it becomes more and more clear that the whole staggering dysfunction of the Karamazovs comes down to this—or, at the very least, this is the root of the problem: the failure to speak the truth about oneself. And if we are not truthful with ourselves, we cannot see our circumstances with clarity and freedom and have some basic or minimal sense of what it is that we must do and are called to do.

Refusing to lie to ourselves does not mean self-deprecation, insisting that "I am a worm." It does not mean that we believe our detractors, who will always be a bit underwhelmed by us. It rather and very simply—oh that it were so simple!—means we see and recognize we have a personal history and experience, we have certain gifts and capacities, we have a certain potential, and that we will speak, and we will act, and we will bring a contribution that is the fruit of a healthy self-confidence. The genius of the striker in soccer is that when all is said and done, those in this role or responsibility know the team is depending on them to take the final touch of the play, and they take that responsibility, they embrace the occasion, and they know how to score. Knowing this—knowing they have the skill to deliver—is not hubris; it is self-knowledge. It is humility to see oneself in truth for the very simple reason that vocation is the stewardship of *this* life.

For all of us—literally, all of us—if we know and live in this freedom, so much depends on parents and teachers. There is no avoiding the extraordinary impact and influence of parents in bringing up a child into and through and beyond adolescence and, hopefully, bringing them to a wise and grace-filled embracing of their individual identity. But there are always others along the way. For myself, I think of Miss Miller in third grade, and then Mr. Veltmeyer in eleventh grade. I also think of the older men who were elders in my life. And of course, there is the gift of friendship—true friendship that loves and does not flatter, that accepts us and encourages us. And we need to speak of marriage. For those who are married, we experience either a continual affirmation through times of set back and discouragement or we find that home itself seems to reinforce our lack of self-esteem. In seeking self-knowledge, it behooves us to look over the landscape of those relationships that have encouraged us on the way, on the track that is consistent with our identity, and identify what we have to bring or offer by way of personal engagement in the work to which we are called.

We will always have the naysayers in our lives. Always. But we can and will find our way if we have those key players who are voting for us—quiet cheerleaders through the transitions of our lives. And if we do not have them, we need to name this and then find them. We cannot navigate this road alone; we must have the companion along the way who is both a source of blessing and accountability. And I should add, we also offer this to others: older men and women to younger men and women, senior colleagues to new appointees, friends who do not flatter but know what it means to say the right thing at the right time. There is hardly a more powerful gift we can give to another.

THE SCOURGE OF NARCISSISM

And yet, we must speak of a danger. We can without doubt affirm the significance and worth of each individual person. But at the same time, we can and must resist narcissism—an engagement with the world fueled by an unhealthy and in-flated sense of our significance. A child naturally experiences the world as revolving around themselves; they are *self-centered*. They feel, and their every perception reinforces this, that they are at the center of the universe and the only thing that happens or that matters is *their* world, including their needs and desires. The only thing that has any meaning is what they experience personally—what they can see and feel and hear. Ideally, of course, we grow up and learn otherwise; we come to see that we are part of a complex system where we do have a part to play, but we also see we are not messiahs, we are not indispensable, we are not heroes. We merely have one contribution to offer, we have one part to play, and we embrace this with humility, alacrity, and grace. The ideal is that our parents would keep our narcissistic tendencies in check. And if they don't, that is why we have siblings! We do not need to have our spirits crushed or broken. Definitely not. But we do need to come to this knowledge—a gracious knowledge: to see ourselves within the whole, as part of (but only one part of) the social systems into which we have come.

We do not need to think of ourselves as particularly special; everyone is special. We do not need to think that somehow we have received a special anointing. We do not need flattery; we do not need everyone to tell us how won-derful we are. One sign of narcissism is the propensity to speak of ourselves as making a unique contribution that is unmatched by any of our predecessors. Surely we do not need to compare ourselves to those who have come before and insist that what we are doing is exponentially better. In soccer, it is the craving to be the GOAT—the "greatest of all time." Why bother with this? Let it go; it is not about you, it is about the team and the sport and the skilled players who have played for many teams and in many situations, and no situation is perfectly comparable to a previous situation. Get over the need to compare. Just ask: In this time and in this place, what part am I being called to play? And if someone insists you are extraordinary, stress that you are part of a system, a community, a team, and that you are only doing your part.

We need affirmation that keeps us true to ourselves and fosters our capacity to contribute to something bigger than ourselves, with grace, humility, wisdom, and the capacity to work effectively with others. But we do not need to think too highly of ourselves; we do not need to overstate our worth or value or the significance of our work. We are merely doing our part. That is, in the words of Romans 12:3, we do not think of ourselves more highly than we ought, but with "sober judgment" we come to see and embrace the way in which we are called to contribute to the greater whole.

It is my "expert" opinion as a grandfather, that grandparents have the unique responsibility to overstate the worth of the artwork of their grandchildren and plaster it all over the refrigerator door. That is our calling with our grandsons and granddaughters; for us, they are awesome and smart and beautiful and strong and the greatest grandchildren ever! But the genius of a father or mother is to see the potential of their son or daughter and to nudge, encourage, open doors and venues for testing their capacity. Many children and young people suffer from an undue level of pressure from their parents to perform—to somehow "make their parents proud" because they are high achievers. We do need to encourage our children; we do need to nudge them to practice and stay the course and do their best. Of course. But most important is to foster a work ethic: a diligence in and about their lives where they know how to play well and then study and read well and then work on a project effectively and enjoy it—to enjoy working with their heads and their hands. In the process, we hopefully discover what it is that most reflects their identity and deepest joy.

But the main point here is that we flee from adulation and flattery and anything that gives undue attention to any contribution we might make. The apostle Paul had no problem affirming his apostolic authority; he did not hesitate to make the case about the content of the Christian gospel. There was no lack of self-confidence in his approach to his life or ministry. But, just as insistently, he refused to overstate his worth or value or significance in the mission of God. When they attempted to foster any kind of cult of personality, he insisted: some plant and some water but in the end, it is God who makes things happen—and that, as he puts it, "we are God's servants, working together" (1 Cor 3:9).

SELF-KNOWLEDGE AND THE LOVE OF GOD

Freedom is found, in part, in seeing and knowing ourselves in truth—a healthy and mature self-awareness—and seeing ourselves as part of a whole. Even if someone is a brilliant pianist, they never achieve their potential without coaching and mentors and the support of complex systems. We know we are dependent on so many to be what we are called to be. And so, we ask, As part of the whole and as contributors alongside others, what do we bring to the table? What do we offer? What skills, capacity, and experience might we bring to this situation or this challenge or this opportunity?

Knowing ourselves is liberating. We unapologetically acknowledge what it is we enjoy doing without the need to impress others or wonder if we are fulfilling their expectations. We can be fully accountable and transparent in our work without the need to impress or be flattered by the other and without fear of criticism. This gives us the freedom to make mistakes and learn from those mistakes. We do not need to falsely project that we have it all together.

But as much as anything, we are freed from any need for comparisons—the inclination to compare ourselves to others as a way to affirm our own worth or significance. We can accept ourselves with certain strengths and with limitations. We can do our part and celebrate the work of others—either colleagues or those who have gone before us. We do not need to boost our own egos by discounting the work of those who preceded us; and we do not need to be threatened by those who might succeed us. We can move through life and work without feeling diminished by others or feeling the need to be more impressive or popular or significant. The sign that we have come to this point in our journey of faith and vocation is that we stop wishing we are anyone other than who we are. We stop making comparisons; we affirm our strengths and limitations. We affirm what it is we might have to offer within this community or organization. We know the grace of being freed from constantly needing to be validated or praised.

There is ultimately only one way we get there. There is only one avenue to this grace, this knowledge, and this freedom: it is to know and believe you are loved—first by your parents and then by others along the way, but in the end to come to that point where you believe and know you are loved by God. You are accepted and forgiven and can dwell in this knowledge—the affective or felt knowledge of the liberating love God has for you and specifically for you. In many respects, this is what it means to know the salvation of God: to know that one is loved—as the apostle puts it, to know "the breadth and length and height and depth, and to know the love of Christ that surpasses knowledge" (Eph 3:18-19).

The liberating power of love gives us the freedom to move beyond pretense; we stop trying to be anyone other than who God made when God made us. We know ourselves and we live graciously in this knowledge. We learn a great deal by imitation—in sports, in the arts, in business, and in teaching and preaching. We learn from the masters who have gone before us. But at some point, we come to a radical realization—radical in that it is fundamental to our sense of self—of our own identity, our own contribution, our own voice. At some point there is a shift for the musician in that he is playing Beethoven through his own skin, or the preacher who has found her own manner of speaking, or the writer who has found his or her own

THE LIBERATING POWER OF LOVE GIVES US THE FREEDOM TO MOVE BEYOND PRETENSE; WE STOP TRYING TO BE ANYONE OTHER THAN WHO GOD MADE WHEN GOD MADE US.

voice. There will always be echoes of those who have gone before us, of course; and yet, the genius of finding ourselves is, in part, that we leave our own mark. Perhaps the image of finding our "voice" applies not merely to writers and preachers and speakers, but to all: self-knowledge is evident, at some point, that we no longer mimic or merely imitate; we no longer are trying to live any other life other than our own. We are freed from pretense. We have found our own voice. We have come to personal coherence and congruence. We live quietly and humbly in the love of God.

WORKING OUT OUR SALVATION

Which leads me to a question. The apostle Paul uses a fascinating phrase in Philippians 2:12 when he calls his readers to "work out your own salvation with fear and trembling." Too frequently, we view this text through the lens of sixteenth century debates between Protestants and Catholics about the significance or non-significance of personal "works" in the salvation of God. But perhaps this way of reading the text misses the point. Perhaps, instead, we should hear this text from a slightly different angle.

Consider that we have been created and redeemed by the gracious work of God, and that we are ultimately only truly saved when we live out the reason for which we were created. This would mean that our salvation is found in doing the work to which we have been called. Our salvation—our knowledge of the love of God—is lived out in this time and in this place very specifically through the work to which we have been called. Our knowledge of the salvation of God is not merely about status (as adopted children) or a matter of position, before God, but much more than that, it is a dynamic. We live infused by and deeply aware of the grace of God—viewed at least, in part, through the lens of our work.

And so, in this time and in this place, we each work out our salvation—that is, in response to the call of God, we live out what it means to know the salvation of God. Vocational holiness is about working out our salvation with fear and trembling—meaning we engage our own lives with a holy and reverent attention, with an appreciation of the weight and gravity of the moment, in the here and now.

Can we speak of vocation as a vehicle or means for our salvation—for what it means to "work out our salvation" with fear and trembling? Yes, of course, it is by faith—deep trust in God—that we come to a knowledge of God's salvation. We are justified by faith; we are not "saved" or vindicated or justified on the basis of any works we perform. We only know the salvation of God if and as we lean into, in trust and dependence, the grace of God. But then our faith in God finds concrete expression in our relationships and in our work—in that through our work we are brought into union with God: we participate with God in the purposes of God for the world and for us in particular. We are "saved" to this end—as we read in Ephesians 2:10—to do the work we were created to do. Thus, our work is not incidental to our knowledge and experience of the salvation of God. Rather our work, our vocation, is a way by which we appropriate and live out what it means to dwell in the salvation of God.

Eugene Peterson writes about the pastoral calling, but what he says actually applies equally to all, regardless of calling, when he observes:

The congregation is the pastor's place for developing vocational holiness ... the place to develop virtue, learn to love, advance in hope. ... The congregation provides the rhythms, the associations, the tasks, the limitations, the temptations—the *conditions*—for this growing up "in every way into him who is the head, into Christ." (Eph 4:15)[2]

To put it differently, our work is a means of our formation—our spiritual formation and thus transformation; it is the means—better, a means—by which we are made whole, restored, and healed. And it is so in part because we are doing what we must do: whether it is parenting this child, drawing this work of art, leading this community-based organization, pastoring this church, starting this business, or teaching this elementary class. We do this and it then becomes the actual here and now of our formation—providing the means, or, as Peterson puts it, the conditions by which we know the transforming grace of God. Our work matters. We do this wholeheartedly and intentionally; we do it knowing the well-being of our souls depends on it. We do it, and in so doing open our hearts to the saving initiative of God in our lives. And in this sense, it is all for our good. We pray, of course, we would be spared any kind of physical or emotional abuse or shaming through our work, but as a rule, everything—both the joys and the trials, both the successes along with the failures and setbacks—is a means by which we know the grace of God.

The bottom line is simply this: vocation is about *this* person at *this* time and in *this* place. Ironically, when all is said and done, it is not about you or me. And yet, we find joy and freedom before God when we learn what it means to be a steward of the life that has been given to us: in this time and in this place.

QUESTIONS FOR REFLECTION AND DISCUSSION

1. Think back to your childhood and teen years—your home and family: Was your home a place of affirmation? Were you pressured to perform in a particular way? Was there acceptance and encouragement with an affirmation of your unique identity?

2. Can you identify an aspect of your work—waged or as a volunteer, in the marketplace or in the church—where you have a keen awareness of how you, specifically *you*, bring what is needed to this place at this time?

3

CALLING AND CALLINGS

THE QUESTION OF VOCATION is never singular. It does not come down to merely asking, "What is my vocation?" as though it is as simple as, "I am called to be an artist . . . or businessperson . . . or pastor." Life is full of multiple callings. Vocation is negotiated through the mix of various obligations, responsibilities, and aspirations.

I am a university administrator, lecturer, writer, grandfather, church member, and neighbor within the community where we live. At any given time and in any given set of circumstances in my life, I need to ask, What is needful in light of all the ways I am being called to be present in this time and this place? What I need to do—what I am *called* upon to do—might arise out of any number of those commitments. In other words, we all live our lives with *multiple* demands, requirements, and responsibilities, all of which we are trying to negotiate and balance.

It is a helpful exercise to list the diverse ways in which you carry obligations and demands on your time and energy. Not only obligations and demands, but those points of investment of time and energy important to you. You volunteer for the local community association because it gives you an opportunity to invest in something that matters to you. A grandchild is born, and you realize "this changes everything"; being a grandparent is now a vital part of your identity and it will alter the way you live your life. You are approached about whether you will be willing to serve on your local church board of elders, and you accept this invitation as an opportunity for service to a faith community that matters to you. So now you have a day job, you are a grandparent, you are involved both in your local church and in the local community, and every part of this matters to you. Sometimes we choose these diverse forms of engagement and responsibility. But other times, they are thrust upon us—an elderly mother falls and is no longer able to live alone, and now the other demands or expectations in our lives need to be put on hold, for the moment at least, while we tend to her immediate and long-term needs. It just has to be done.

Sometimes these multiple callings are in tension or actual conflict. You might be a student or a writer, and you are working on a manuscript deadline. You have a day left to complete it and then learn early that morning that your daughter is sick and has to stay home from school. Your work as a father suddenly "interfered," one might say, with the calling to get the writing project completed. Or consider the man who decided he would not go into a particular field of medicine because he knew the demands of that specialty would mean he could not be fully present to his children. Or the single mother who feels called to be an artist; she so wishes she had time to be present to her small corner of the living room she calls her studio, but she is the only wage earner for this little family and there is no avoiding this nor any desire to not be a mother and caregiver for her children.

At other times, however, these multiple callings are not in conflict but rather in dynamic tension. Jacques Ellul was a university professor teaching law, an active member of his local city council, a theologian, and a writer. No doubt there were times when he felt these were in tension, for many of us his life was lived out as an integrated whole. For example, his calling to serve on the city council deeply informed his work as a theologian and writer. He could not be the one without the other. This "also"—"I am a father, on the local church board, and *also* heading up my own business"—is captured so well in the apt title of a book by Bonnie Miller-McLemore titled *Also a Mother*.[1]

Whether in actual conflict or in dynamic tension, whether we have chosen these multiple commitments or they are just part of the vicissitudes of life and work—it is the "also" in Miller-McLemore's title that needs to be considered: to reflect on how we navigate and negotiate multiple "alsos" as we seek to be present and faithful stewards of our lives in the here and now, in this time and in this place.

TENDING THE INNER CIRCLE

One helpful way to consider what it means to have multiple callings is by thinking in terms of three concentric circles.[2] Each concentric circle represents something that is important—some aspect of who you are and what you are called to be and do. The innermost circle is the absolute "must do"—it is important, urgent, and essential. It is nonnegotiable. The second circle—the middle segment—consists of those action items that are important and to some degree essential, but not as pressing. They need to be done; at some point they need to happen if we are going to be faithful to our identity and life purpose, but they can only happen if the inner circle is tended. And in the third circle are those items that matter to you, but you know you can only get to them when you have on some level satisfied the demands and requirements of the two inner circles.

The inner circle is where we must begin, and it can be thought of in two ways. For some, the inner circle essentially pays the rent. If it is something you enjoy and is also consistent with what you most feel called to do, great. That is good news. But for many, if not for most, that inner circle is simply that which needs to happen to keep the roof over our heads, food on the table, and the boss at least minimally happy. Ask yourself, What do I simply have to do at this point—today or as the priority of my life for the here and now? It may well be that other things—important no doubt—have to be set aside because something is pressing that simply has to be done. If you are the pastor of a church, you might well have many things you want to do and plan to do, but you need a sermon for the upcoming Sunday service, or you have a board meeting and a report is due. In both cases, it is not a matter of what you want to do or feel like doing; you know your responsibilities mean there is something that has to be tended to. It may be the mere mundane: this is laundry day and it has to be done. Or it may be that on the horizon you have a due date for a writing or art project, and to that end you do today what needs to be done today so you can meet that commitment by the agreed-upon deadline.

Second, the inner circle is also that which happens now, or it simply does not happen. The farmer plants in the spring and harvests in the fall. That is when it must happen. Your child is home from school sick and requires your full-time attention. Or you discover the roof has a leak and so it cannot be put off; it has to be repaired now.

When my sons were thirteen and fifteen, a wise older man and I were on a walk. We chatted about my life circumstances, and he was genuinely interested in my various projects. He was pleased to know I had some speaking invitations coming my way. But then he graciously noted, "Don't forget, Gordon, that your sons will be thirteen and fifteen only once and you only get one chance to be a father to them in their early teens. You will have plenty of speaking opportunities down the road, but . . ." Well, he did not need to finish the sentence. I heard him loud and clear. He was simply eager to impress on me that being a father was an "inner circle" priority; if it mattered to me, as he knew it did, it was nonnegotiable.

Perhaps you are a professor in a college or university. And for all the items on your to-do list, you know you need to be ready for the coming semester—specifically the courses you are scheduled to teach. Whether it is the pastor who is preparing for the coming Sunday, or the professor who has courses lined up, or the salesperson who knows there is a quota of sales to be met, each one knows what it means to pay the rent. It has to happen. In your work—whatever that might be—it is helpful to be very clear about what, week to week, is expected and required; if this does not happen, you will not get a contract renewal or keep your job. It is clearly located within your inner circle.

THE SECOND AND THIRD CIRCLES

It is helpful to think of the second circle as something vitally important—but it is of second order priority in terms of time commitment. The fact that you place it in the second circle does not mean it does not have as much significance or that it matters to you any less. For some, it may well be that where they feel most aligned to their sense of personal call is actually in this circle. But it is not pressing in the sense that it pays the rent or demands our immediate attention.

And yet, it needs to happen. For some, it will be something you tend to every day—or most days, at least—that reflects something that needs to happen but might only be done in small increments. Anthony Trollope—the nineteenth-century English novelist best known, perhaps, for *Barchester Towers*—is famous in part for his daily writing routines and disciplines. Early morning before he headed off to his paid employment as a civil servant working for the postal service, he would write with a focus that required he put down 250 words in quarter-hour free times during his day. I try to imagine this pace happening in the days before the laptop computer keyboard. This man was writing longhand! He ended up publishing forty-seven novels along with a string of plays, essays, and articles. He did it in fifteen-minute segments alongside what we speak of as his "day job."

This approach to life and work and vocation is perhaps best captured by the line attributed to Emile Zola—Italian and then French novelist, essayist, and journalist—who insisted that he needed to write every day. He did so over the course of thirty years with the guiding mantra: *nulla dies sine linea*— not a day without a line. I can attest to this personally. My own writing is important to me, but it is not my "day job"; it does not pay the rent. And yet, I am so very grateful for the advice from a friend who back in my twenties urged me to find a way to write every day—even if it was a very full and demanding day. While I certainly do not always achieve this objective, it has and is happening with enough regularity.

Ask yourself the question: In order for me to be faithful to who I am and what I must do, what needs to be tended or scheduled or happening alongside the items already listed in the inner circle? It may not be anything more than an hour a day. You are a single mother and the only wage earner for your family, and the only time you have to draw and paint is late evening after your children are in bed. But we cannot underestimate what can happen over the long term from nothing more than an hour a day. A writer may not put down any more than five hundred to one thousand words a day. An artist may feel the first fifteen minutes of that single hour each day is spent setting up again, and again, and again. But you stay the course. You persist. You get into a daily rhythm and routine and, in time, you move the dial.

The second of the three concentric circles can be thought of as those items that are important—they need to happen— but life goes on if they do not happen. At least if they don't happen immediately. The inner circle holds the nonnegotiables; the second circle contains those things that have to be done—the lawn needs to be mowed, the squeaky door needs to be greased, the flight needs to be booked for upcoming travel. They need to be done, but things are only desperate if they are left to the last minute.

The second circle might be thought of this way: The dishes need to be done, no doubt about it; they cannot be stacked indefinitely. But for now, they can wait. Those who are serious about the inner circle will always have those matters that need to be done but which they know how to set aside and put on hold because something else that is a vocational imperative has to be done.

The third circle is where we place those action items that may well be quite good to do but which are clearly in the category of, we do them if and only if there is time, and as and only as there is time. They are the things which we would like very much to be able to do. But we know in the grand scheme of things we have to pay the rent and we need to tend to that which is essential to our lives—either the job for which we are contracted and employed or the basic needs of our household.

NEGOTIATING THE TENSIONS

Managing what lies within these three concentric circles will not be easy. We will always be navigating tensions, stress points, perhaps even what Greg Jones speaks of as "conflicting senses of vocation to which we are called," competing and legitimate claims on our lives, on our time, and thus on our sense of vocation.[3] Part of what it means to be human and Christian is that there is limited time; we cannot do everything we would like to do. And, further, inherent in our calling is that we defer, we let go, we sacrifice for the sake of the other—for our neighbor, for our children, for the organizations of which we are a part, or the church community that matters to us. And yet the tension is that it is never only about sacrifice; we must—absolutely must—sustain some sense of our self, of our innermost sensibilities and joys, and of those things we simply must do if we are faithful to our own sense of calling and vocation—if we are stewards of our lives.

Thus, we have this tension. It may be that we constantly feel torn about our many pressure points and various expectations. Perhaps we live with this nagging thought of something we would perhaps very much like to do and want to do but simply do not have the time to do.

> **WE MUST SUSTAIN SOME SENSE OF OUR SELF, OF OUR INNERMOST SENSIBILITIES AND JOYS.**

Having said as much, we must emphasize that we can only manage this tension if we are clear about the inner circle: what must be done, what pays the rent.

Here is the key to the inner circle. We just do it, with minimal, if any, grumbling. We cannot live with perpetual resentment that our innermost circle either takes up all our time, or that we wish we had more time. We live graciously in time, and each day and each season of our lives assures that those items that belong in our inner circle are there and tended; they receive an appropriate level of our time and attention.

As a side note, there is something that needs to be added here: we might have something in that inner circle that does not need to be there. There is a helpful phrase I believe comes from the Ignatian spiritual tradition: "misguided generosity." We all want to be generous. In our workplace, we all want to be diligent and thorough, working hard and earning our keep and making a contribution. Within our family systems, we want to be a faithful and engaged parent or, when our parents move into their senior years, to be present and attentive to their needs.

But a distinction needs to be made between an appropriate level of generosity and diligence—faithful and hard-working and present to others—and a generosity that arises out of good intentions but is not truly reflective of our responsibility and calling. It is not a responsibility we are called to bear. And here we ask ourselves, What are we doing, perhaps even daily—or if not daily, often enough—that, if we are honest with ourselves, is outside the scope of what is needful? We do it because we want the reputation of being hard working and thorough, or because we cannot bear the thought that someone who wants a daily visit will think we do not love them anymore. We do not want the social discomfort of saying to our aging mother, "I am going to visit you twice a week, Mother," and, "It will no longer be daily." I am not for a moment suggesting you should not visit your mother each day in the seniors' complex. I am merely asking the question: What is needful? What does she *actually* need from you? It may be impressive that you are on the church board for twenty years continuously, but at what point might it have been wise to say, "I have done my part, made a contribution, and now I can let others be involved; I will step aside not only to let others be involved but because I need to invest my time and energy elsewhere." This means, of course, that we know how to say no. We cannot say yes to that which is most congruent with our lives and our callings if we are not able to say no.

Let me stress this: there is no vocational focus, no vocational integrity and commitment, no capacity to truly engage the here and now without the ability to say no. Without doubt, we need to ask ourselves if our no reflects a lack of generosity or if we do not want to say yes because it would mean doing something dif-

> **WE CANNOT SAY YES TO THAT WHICH IS MOST CONGRUENT WITH OUR LIVES AND OUR CALLINGS IF WE ARE NOT ABLE TO SAY NO.**

ficult or something that would make us uncomfortable but which is, indeed, something we should do. We need to ask that question. But then, with clarity on that score, we need to just say no. And we need to say no when we mean no. We do not need to obfuscate or deflect or say "I'll get back to you" when we know the answer is no, or blame someone else or even claim we are too busy or that the timing is not right or anything else that is merely a lack of clarity and simplicity of speech and communication.

And the converse also applies, of course; we need to be the kind of people to whom others can simply say they are not able or available to respond to our request. We refuse to harangue or use emotional blackmail or anything else to get our way; we need to allow others to say no to us.

Wise women and men tend the inner circle; they guard it and protect the time and energy they give to that which is of the highest priority in their life and work. They pay the rent; they do what must be done on this day. And they also tend to the second circle. They find the space in their days— even if only very minimal time—to keep at that which is central or essential to their vocation or calling. Few things are so crucial when it comes to vocational integrity and clarity as tending the inner circle and finding space for some of what is found in our second circle. We do not reduce our lives to that inner circle; we are just clear about what is found there and what must remain there. And then, as noted, what needs to complement that inner circle so that something important to us is sustained—that which is found in that second circle.

ASKING THE RIGHT QUESTIONS

In all of this, it is helpful to respond to six questions that shape and inform how we spend our time and, more to the point, how we navigate our multiple callings.

First question: What do I need to do today because the circumstances demand it? Whether because it pays the rent or because of the season when the planting needs to happen, or because of what I see on the horizon in my calendar, this is when this needs to happen.

This needs to be front and center in your thinking and in your sense of call. For the here and now, what needs to have your energy, time, and attention? This includes asking what it means not merely for today but then also asking, In this season or chapter of my life and work—in the here and now—what needs to happen? To be at home with a sick child. To tend to an aging mother. To just accept that this is what I need to do and must do as a parent, as a good Samaritan, or because this is what I am contracted to do—even though it may not give me a lot of joy, it needs to be done.

Second question: Where do I find that something is being neglected or put to one side because of procrastination? If there is something that needs to be tended to, but there is an inner hesitation or block or resistance, why not just name it? Call it what it is: procrastination. And then ask, What is it that is keeping me from doing what I know I should be doing?

Third question: To what do I need to be saying no? There are any number of times we feel pressured to say yes when we should be saying no: the expectations of others, perhaps, or things we would love to be able to do. When you say yes to something but know on some level that you should have said no, consider stepping back and asking, Why did I say yes? What was the pressure point—perhaps some sort of emotional blackmail? Or perhaps a desire to be liked and not disappoint someone who matters to us? Or perhaps we said yes because it would bring short-term gratification of some kind. Then have a conversation partner where this is stated out loud, as a kind of confession, so that you grow in your capacity to say no when saying no is the right response to an opportunity or pressure point. Keep this in mind: if we do not say no, we are not saying yes to that which is most important and essential.

Fourth question: What does it mean for me to be attentive to that which feeds my soul and my sense of self? One way to come at this is to insist we do not lose—in the midst of all these callings—a sense of self. What deep sensibility informs our work and gives integrity to all the things we are called to do? Dorothy Day was—at heart—a journalist. Another person might recognize that in the midst of all she does, she is fundamentally a gardener. Personally, I am a theologian—even when I am giving institutional leadership to a university, it is still an exercise in meaning-making (that is the work of a theologian). Another might be first and foremost a teacher. Or a pastor. Thomas Merton was a writer; even as a monk, in a secluded monastic community, he could not *not* write. He was both a monk and a writer; and, thankfully, the abbot of the monastery recognized this and gave Merton time to write. This knowledge of one's deep sensibility can serve as something of a compass as one navigates various or diverse callings.

And on this fourth question, what must not be missed is that often that aspect of our calling or vocation might be done at the margins of the demands and expectations of our circumstances. Perhaps it is to say, "Yes, I have 101 demands on my time, but I will insist that each day I will write—I will find a window in the day and put down two hundred or one thousand words: *nulla dies sine linea*—not a day without a line." Or, "Every day I will find space to draw or head to the garden to weed, even if it is only for thirty minutes." Yes, we are called to give up our lives for the sake of the neighbor, and yes, we are called to give ourselves in radical and sacrificial service for the other. But we can only do this if we tend to our personal well-being—nurturing our sense of self, what is most crucial to our identity and vocation so that, actually, we have something to give when we serve others.

A fifth question: What compulsion or activity or investment of time and energy is keeping us from something that should be tended? For myself, I know that part of the answer is that I like to have the reputation that if you send me an email, you will get a prompt reply—within twenty-four hours or forty-eight hours at the most. But where does this compulsion come from? What obligates me to do this? Why does it matter to me so much? And, if this is what I am doing, what is not happening that should be happening instead? Why not simply know that I will respond, in due time, but not feel this (misguided?) compulsion to answer on the other person's timeline rather than on my own. I say that fully appreciating that some email messages are part of the inner circle and require a prompt response: from the chair of the university board of governors to whom I report, from my sons and their wives, and, of course, from my grandchildren!

But then also, it was sobering, a number of years ago, to realize how many hours each week I was spending watching professional sports: ice hockey (I am a Canadian, after all), but also baseball if my favorite team was in the playoffs, and soccer every chance I got, but especially during UEFA Euro and the World Cup. And no surprise, it added up. There is certainly much joy in sharing in the ups and downs of our local teams with family and friends; I am merely saying that we need to tend to what matters most.

And then, a sixth question. There will be a tension between our various and multiple callings. As we consider the demands and limits of time, the pressure between what is demanded of us, and what pulls us one way or the other, consider this: Is there a way in which one calling informs and gives meaning to another? There is an interesting publication where the editors ask what it means for someone to be called to be both an academic and a parish priest—looking specifically to the Anglican Church in England.[4] The premise of this series of essays is that some have this dual calling and that it may be quite fruitful to think of both sides—the academic and the parish ministry—as distinct but also as each giving perspective to the other. In other words, when we feel a tension between two dimensions or aspects or expressions of our lives, is there a sense that one informs and gives enhanced meaning to the other? Years ago, I read an interview with Rowan Williams, and he spoke of how his writing and scholarly work was not a distraction or impediment to his work as Archbishop of the Church of England; rather, he insisted that he served as archbishop *as* one who wrote.

Can one's work as a mother or caregiver or librarian inform one's "other" work as an artist or writer or designer? Is there a way to think of one dimension of our working as giving meaning and nuance to another side of our identity and calling? I am a university administrator and a grandfather. This does not mean I am always ready and willing to show off photos of my grandchildren—though I am—as my experience as a grandfather is not an impediment or conflict to my work as president. Rather, the call to be a tender presence to these young women and men cultivates within me, I hope, a similar disposition toward those I am called to serve within the university.

This may not always be the case; sometimes our two worlds need to be kept distinct. Bivocational pastors may well find one side of their calling informs the other, but this does not mean a pastor—in business while also giving pastoral leadership to a church, for example—always illustrates in sermons from the experience of running a family business. There is a place to keep the two distinct. And yet, we can be alert, even if it is a quiet and understated relationship, to how there is a dynamic tension, even an organic connection, between one calling we have and another.

Mary Catherine Bateson speaks to this in her reflections titled *Composing a Life*. She suggests that life is always a series of improvisations—a work in progress—where we are making sense of our lives in the midst of competing demands, conflicting priorities. There are unforeseen developments and smaller or greater crises that inevitably come our way. The genius of a life well lived is that we find congruence and meaning, not despite all of this but precisely in the midst of what she speaks of as a "complex ecosystem," meaning we live with ambiguity—rather than following a single life vision, we learn to embrace "multiplicity."[5]

Each of these six questions comes up again and again in our lives as we learn what it means to navigate our multiple callings. When it comes to learning what it means to say no, for example, we will not always get it right. There will be times when we said no and later saw that we should have done it; our heart was not in the right place when we declined to do something. And just as often, there will be times in which we agreed to be somewhere or do something, and we realize afterward it was not what was required of us or needed. We learn from our miscues and, over time, grow in our capacity to navigate the diverse dimensions of our lives with grace, patience, and fruitfulness.

EMBRACING OBSCURITY

Finally, consider that in managing all of these circles—these diverse or multiple callings—sooner or later we come to see that we are ultimately only faithful in our identity and vocation if and as we learn what it means to be content with obscurity. Some of the most important work we will do will be done behind the scenes. It is done because it needs to be done, but it will not be work for which we get affirmation, recognition, or thanks. We just do it because we care for others—whether family or church or the organization where we work or are employed. Our work is never only that which is public. Our work is not one and the same as what others can see and affirm.

We can, as part of our vocation, be in prayer for others; but we do not need to announce to them that we are praying for them. We just do it. The carpenter may spend hours on one particular project and stays the course because the work matters, whether or not credit is given for a particular task or focus. A scholar is diligent on her sources; an archivist in the basement is very particular about how things are filed and will not know thanks because in the end the person who takes advantage of these archives will not even know who did this work.

> THE LONGING FOR AFFIRMATION AND PRAISE CAN SO EASILY DISTRACT US FROM THE GOOD WORK TO WHICH WE ARE CALLED, THE GOOD WORK THAT NEEDS TO BE DONE.

And I wonder the following: Could it be that

there is only integrity in our vocation or calling if and as we have at least some aspect of what we do that is merely done because it needs to be done? The pastor does what needs to be done and does not feel the need to let the congregation or the board know what happened. It merely happened; it was done because it needed to be done. The reason I offer this thought is that the longing for affirmation and praise can so easily distract us from the good work to which we are called, the good work that needs to be done. So, we starve this craving by doing that which needs to be done—with diligence and care. Perhaps every day there is something on the to-do list that is in this category—something that just needs doing. And what it does is bring an integrity to the whole of who we are and what we are called to be and do.

QUESTIONS FOR REFLECTION AND DISCUSSION

1. What do I need to do today because the circumstances of my life and work require it?

2. What am I neglecting because I am simply procrastinating?

3. To what do I need to say no—what are the requests or expectations I do not need to say yes to?

4. What do I need to tend to because it feeds my soul?

5. What compulsion or time-consuming activity is perhaps keeping me from that which matters most?

6. In what way may one of my callings actually strengthen and inform some other aspect of how I have been called?

4

CAREER TRANSITIONS

NEW DIRECTIONS, NEW ORIENTATIONS

AT THE OFFICE, there is a search underway to replace a person who is retiring. In anticipation of the formal interviews, I reviewed the CV (curriculum vitae) of an applicant to see what would catch my attention and what questions I might ask when we are face to face with the candidate. Typically, when we look at a CV, we look for a story, a career progression, perhaps a sequence of roles and responsibilities. Yes, we certainty look at education and formal training that would be relevant for the position. But as much as anything, we are looking at the trajectory: Has this person passed through the logical sequence that would lead one to think they are ready for the position for which they are being interviewed? Has this candidate gained experience in a more junior post, perhaps, so they can now assume a role with greater responsibility?

But, what about another narrative? What about the person who has stepped out of what we might think of as the typical sequence of the career they have had and moved into something quite different? That is, I wonder about those peripheral moves—something that might emerge as a bit of a surprise, even. They sell the business and go into a line of work that is much different; they take an early retirement from one career so they can devote their energies to something quite in contrast to what they have been doing.

For those who make this move, there is typically a deeper and underlying logic. There is no doubt there are some who have questioned their decision and wondered why they would do something so opposite the expected course of things. But consider that there is a logic; and that there are certain times when we need to affirm and celebrate those who have the courage to make such a move and recognize that this does happen—that God's calling often takes a person in a new and perhaps surprising direction.

THE ALTERNATE APPROACH TO LIFE AND CAREER

We typically think of career as a series of logical steps—a sequence. We apprentice within a field, then we join a team—perhaps as a junior member of the firm. Next, we move into a more senior role, and over time we are a partner, if not actually the senior member of the organization. Then we move into a mentoring role to those who are in the apprentice mode, and we pass on the wisdom we have learned in both the successes and disappointments along the way.

Those on a pastoral track typically join a staff as an assistant pastor—the most junior role. In time, they become associate pastor, and then a senior pastor to a smaller congregation, and eventually the senior pastor of a larger congregation with a multi-staff. Or an academic: the first appointment is as a lecturer, perhaps, then they become an assistant professor. In time, they are promoted to associate and then eventually to full professor. Quite possibly, they become the head of the department, maybe even a dean of the faculty. Some might become the president of the college or the university. There is a logical sequence through the profession. This sequence is as often as not evident on a résumé. And when we hire, we assume if one is applying for a vice president role, it is because they have been a director or manager or senior team member and now they are ready for the lead role on the team—leveraging their experience and all they have learned on the job so they can assume the next logical step in their career.

Some even map this out; they know where they want to be in a decade, and they do what it takes to position themselves for the next step in the progression to the most senior position within their field.

But what about those who choose to step out of this seemingly logical sequence of their professions or careers? Can we speak about those who in midlife, perhaps their mid-forties or midfifties, choose to resign or take an early retirement in order to do something different—perhaps *very* different. Their story, their vocational narrative, may include a significant surprise or two along the way. They have made a peripheral move, sideways, one might say. This is not merely a bend in the road or a slight detour; they have made a sharp turn. Actually, they have chosen a completely different path and done so when as often as not they were at the top of their craft. They did not need to make the move for financial reasons or because they were not successful at what they were doing. They made the move because of a sense of vocation: the new direction is a calling.

In what follows, I admit I have a particular interest in the calling to religious leadership and pastoral ministry within Christian congregations. I observe there is a declining sense of call among young people—high school students and university students—a call, that is, to ordained Christian ministry. But at the same time, we must note, increasingly there are those who are making a midcareer transition from business, education, and other fields into pastoral leadership. If this is what is emerging, this is potentially a very good thing. The most notable example of this is likely the current Archbishop of Canterbury, the Most Reverend Justin Welby, who spent eleven years in the oil and gas industry, mainly in France, before pursing theological studies toward ordination within the Church of England. But the main observation is that we can find this happening in so many spheres of life and work—the pastor who retires early to focus on painting and art, the school teacher who accepts an appointment to serve as the children's ministry pastor in her local church, the empty-nest mother who joins a colleague to run a small business, the businessperson who accepts an assignment to head up a nonprofit community development project.

This is not possible in every endeavor or field or occupation. If you want to get into professional ballet dancing, you cannot decide in your midforties that you missed your call and now you need to give "ballerina" a go. The window of opportunity may have been lost. This would apply to most athletic and artistic endeavors. But in so many spheres of involvement, there are windows of opportunity to make transitions and to embrace a role or responsibility or occupation as a relative newcomer to this line of work and to do this in midlife.

MOTIVATIONS AND DISTINCT CIRCUMSTANCES

People make midcourse or midcareer transitions for a whole host of reasons—potentially very different motivations. That is, the occasion or the catalyst for this kind of midlife move could be very different from one person to another. For some, it comes as a chance to finally do what all along they knew and have known they needed to do. Finally, the time has come; they have been waiting or, in some cases, denying their first love and now they are ready to embrace it. Perhaps they are primary home givers and not until they are in their forties can they now devote the time and energy to this calling or work they view to be so vital to their sense of identity. Maybe there were financial or economic pressures limiting them from making this move. But now they can take early retirement, and with a modest pension make the shift and begin to do what they must do and eagerly want to do.

It is interesting to meet those who make this midcareer shift when they are a little older and have known all along that they were not quite in alignment with their true calling. For some of these, there is no doubt there were family pressures and expectations. I think of the thirty-nine-year-old physician—hearing him tell his story of how his grandfather was a doctor and his father was a family doctor and how it was always assumed through his childhood and teen years that this would be his calling as well. Much was made of this in the narrative of his home: that he would take up the baton, this fine legacy. Any thought or suggestion that he would not be a physician was hardly contemplated, in that it would be thought to be a kind of betrayal of the wonderful heritage he had—almost a betrayal of these predecessors. As he tells his story, he concludes with a very simple statement: "But it is not me."

Family pressure might be one such impediment to embracing a vocation sooner. But there are any number of factors that might blur one's vision and keep one from seeing and recognizing one's calling. So yes, in some cases, a person may have known all along that they chose their direction as a young person, but they have had this nagging sense that the motivation was not the best. Perhaps it was the pursuit of financial security. Economics will be a factor in vocational discernment, but in time many come to see the pursuit of wealth and financial security took on an inordinate weight—the only thing they could see.

Whatever it was—family expectations, the pursuit of financial security, or other factors (or a combination of factors)—they did not in their youth embrace their calling. They did not do what they were actually called to do; perhaps like the proverbial Jonah, they knew their calling but intentionally went another way. But more often than not, those pressure points kept them from seeing and having the courage to embrace their calling.

So yes, some had a calling earlier, but they did not see it; or, if they did see it, did not have the grace and courage and

> SOME HAD A CALLING EARLIER, BUT THEY DID NOT SEE IT; OR IF THEY DID SEE IT, DID NOT HAVE THE GRACE AND COURAGE AND SUPPORTING CIRCUMSTANCES TO MAKE THE STEP.

supporting circumstances to actually make the step. As a side note, it is helpful to see how a family system and a religious subculture foster a narrative that inherently excludes some possibilities. Perhaps the arts are not taken seriously—if not actually discounted—with a subtle or less than subtle narrative that no one in their right mind would be an artist. Or perhaps in another home there is a similar dismissiveness to any inclination a young person might have for going into business or into the trades because parents want their children to be in certain professions. And religious communities can put similar pressure points on a young person with a narrative that highlights and legitimizes certain callings or occupations and dismisses others. Girls are socialized into a particular way of viewing their involvement in the world, and they would be hard pressed to get out of that social construct. And it might be years later that a young woman has someone come into her life who opens up a new possibility—for her to be a business entrepreneur, or a sculptor, or a theologian, or a pastor. Or a friend of mine for whom the pressure to go into pastoral ministry was so intense—to please parents and fulfill the aspirations of his religious community—but after struggling in the pastorate, found freedom in finally accepting his calling into business where he has flourished.

All of that to say that some missed their calling when they were younger and now, in midcareer they see it, and they are now positioned to embrace who it is they are called to be. But I wonder the following: Could it be that for some this trajectory is actually providential? That is, that the young person was very much called into business or the arts or into public school teaching and now, in midlife, is responding to a new and emerging expression of their identity? They did not miss their calling; rather, now, in midlife, they see that what they have been doing was preparation and anticipation for what is emerging next for them? Such a person was perhaps very much called into pastoral office and ministry with a deep love for and commitment to the local church and only later made a transition to be an academic or a writer or the director of a nonprofit agency. The seeds of what emerged later were there all along; but now those seeds have germinated. In midlife this person comes to see that however much what they have been doing was good and appropriate and what they were called to do, they now have an opportunity to make a transition—not as a denial of their previous identity and work but as a new opportunity. This new opportunity may not seem to be the logical sequence to others, but one they have come to see as very much who they are and what they are called to be and do. A classic example is that of Moses, who at age eighty was tending sheep in the desert when he was called to return to the center of the action and be the liberator for his fellow people. This did not come out of the blue; he was uniquely qualified for this role and responsibility. His whole life had prepared him for this, and yet, only now had the time come to take up the mantel of this essential work.

To those in midlife for whom this might be the case, we need people in our lives who nudge, encourage, and call this out of us. We need to ask if there is something percolating that should be named and acknowledged. Are colleagues and friends making asides—comments and observations—that reflect they see something we need to also acknowledge? Are people who know us well saying such things as: "What you do, you do well, but have you ever thought of . . . this or that or the other?" That is, to those in mid or later in life, we need to ask them, Is there a movement within your heart that you, at the very least, need to attend to and ask what it means and find a way to test and see if this is of God?

Perhaps you take a summer to consider this possibility. You take a theology or Scripture course at a seminary and wonder if you have a calling to religious leadership. Or you head off for a two-week summer school excursus at a school of art—a summer program where you might be the oldest one there, but it gives you an opportunity to see if this is your true métier. Or you join up on a short-term mission trip that leaves you knowing you are to sell your business and move from being in business to heading up a team in the community development world. Or maybe a friend

> **IS THERE A MOVEMENT WITHIN YOUR HEART THAT YOU NEED TO ATTEND TO AND ASK WHAT IT MEANS AND FIND A WAY TO TEST AND SEE IF THIS IS OF GOD?**

who has a growing business needs an extra hand and asks you to work with her for a couple of months. And it gives you a chance to ask, Is this something I might be called to be and do?

The point is that midcareer or mid-course realignments and new directions are potentially a vital part of our lives, thus a key means by which we live out our vocations in the here and now.

FROM EXPERT TO BEGINNER

A midcareer move, while potentially a very good thing, requires we have a particular sensibility and emotional capacity. Actually, consider two perspectives simultaneously. First, ask what expertise you bring to the table, to this new role, so you can leverage your previous experience within a new context or sphere of responsibilities. If you have been a public school teacher and you are moving into pastoral ministry, you recognize and affirm that this experience as a schoolteacher means you bring an invaluable perspective into the work of religious leadership.

And yet, you are making the change and entering into a sphere of engagement, a craft, a manner of being, that is likely a very different world. If you move from business into pastoral ministry, you do not run the church like a business. If you go from the pastorate into business or into community development or into the academic, you bring all that pastoral experience into the new setting, certainly, but your clients or your students are not your parishioners. You are making a transition that requires recognizing two things: first, the need for a new set of capacities; and second, there is an adjustment that comes with entering into a different organizational culture.

When it comes to your skills, capacities, and expertise, there is no avoiding that you are a rookie; you are a junior member of the team even if you are the oldest one in the room. Those who make midcourse transitions are often leaving a position where they may well be at the top of their game. They have mastered the art of innovation and entrepreneurship in business and moved into a senior role within a company or within their own business venture. They have excelled in the work of pastoral ministry and leadership and are now making the transition into the academy. And now, they are the newbies—they are finding their way like much younger colleagues. They feel they are a junior member of the team. They will catch up soon enough; but starting out, they are rookies, and they will not bring a veteran's touch to this new position or assignment.

In so many fields of work and engagement, doing something again and again and again, over many years, is the only way to master a craft. Good preachers are not great preachers until they have preached hundreds of sermons over the course of many years. And when you move into pastoral ministry in midcareer, you are doing something as a beginner that your peers have been at for twenty or more years. As noted, you will catch up soon enough; but starting out, it can be humbling as you try to figure it all out. If you are moving from business into pastoral ministry, the role of elders and the character of church politics is a very different world from a corporate leadership team. If you have been your own boss, it might be quite the challenge to now have a church board or an academic dean holding you accountable. If you move into the political sphere, run for office, and arrive in the legislature, you may be coming out of the business world where you made the strategic decisions, and now you have to be part of a bipartisan deliberative exercise. You will be side by side with others who have likely by now mastered this world and this way of getting things done.

The key in all of this? Stay humble, keep your sense of humor, be a learner—without any apology, be a learner. Nell Irvin Painter, an accomplished historian and professor at Princeton University, forthrightly speaks of the challenges of being an older person making a start in a new field in *Old in Art School: A Memoir of Starting Over*, where she stresses that in making a transition, one must be a learner.[1]

> **STAY HUMBLE, KEEP YOUR SENSE OF HUMOR, BE A LEARNER—WITHOUT ANY APOLOGY, BE A LEARNER.**

And learn you must. Do not assume that your expertise in another field immediately translates into this new assignment. If you are going into business, sign up for an Executive MBA—studying on weekends and evenings. If you are coming from business and now serving in the senior administration of a university—perhaps as CFO—then make it intentional that you will learn the culture and the way decisions are made and how finances are managed in a nonprofit organization. If you are heading from business into pastoral ministry, then get started: study theology and Scripture and the history of pastoral practice. Perhaps you do an entire Master of Divinity through modular and online course options—though an ideal would be to take a sabbatical for some focused study time as you make the transition to the new role or responsibility. It can be a challenge if it has been over twenty years since you were in a classroom. But being later to the table does not mean you do not need to do your homework.

In other words, do not assume you can merely leverage past experience and that will be sufficient—that life experience is all that is required or that experience in one line of work is qualification enough for this new assignment. That is the genius of the transition: to leverage and draw on our past experiences, and the strengths and capacities we have developed while *also* coming into the new role and responsibility as a learner.

I have two valued colleagues who moved from their senior roles as pastors of prominent congregations into teaching roles on the faculty of graduate theological schools. Both of them were accomplished veteran and respected pastors. We offered them their teaching appointments because they were obviously successful and effective as pastors. But when they arrived, they were suddenly rookies in this new environment; they were now working with everything from faculty meeting politics to how to work with a dean in the design of their courses. They were moving from the top of their game to a situation where they were newcomers. They were very gracious in that they were now just one of the gang, with their offices down the hall with other faculty— no longer holding the corner office, so to speak. But they chose to work from within, learn the culture, and leverage their strengths alongside colleagues toward a vision for the mission of, in this case, a theological seminary.

I think of the pastor who becomes a pastor after over twenty years in business. Or the schoolteacher who, at age fifty-five, accepts and responds to a calling into congregational leadership and ministry. Or the business executive who decides she is first and foremost an artist and that this is what she must do. So, she sells the business and converts her garage into a studio. Yes of course, she will leverage her business background to tend to the economic side of her new focus. Each of these, of course, will leverage the experience and expertise they bring to the new situation. But if you move from business into pastoral ministry or into academic leadership, this does not mean that as a pastor or an academic you now run the church or the university like a for-profit business. That point must be made and made again. Yes, you can and surely must bring to the new role the insights, wisdom, and experience from your earlier life that can be leveraged for this new role. And yet, you come as a rookie with a humble willingness to learn.

Somewhere (I am not sure where), T. S. Eliot made the passing remark that with God there is no wasted time. We need to keep this perspective in mind—regardless of the terms or conditions by which

WITH GOD THERE IS NO WASTED TIME.

we came into a midcareer transition. For some, as noted, they "missed" their call because they refused to see it or, in seeing it, feared to embrace it and acknowledge it, or because of family pressures or expectations. For others, this was all providential; they did not receive the call into the new line of work until midlife. Either way the principle remains: with God there is no wasted time. So without regrets about the past, we embrace the new opportunity with alacrity, courage, and humility—graciously accepting that we are new to a role but also unapologetically leveraging the experience and expertise cultivated or developed in the earlier chapters of our lives and work.

QUESTIONS FOR REFLECTION AND DISCUSSION

1. Think of someone you know who has made a peripheral move successfully—that is, someone who in midcareer or later made the transition. What stands out to you from their experience?

2. For yourself, is there the potential to make such a move? Something you have wanted to do, perhaps? Or is it that you just need the nudge, the encouragement, the support, or the training to make the transition?

5

TENDING TO THE
LIFE OF THE MIND

REGARDLESS OF OUR VOCATION—WHETHER in religious work, business, the arts, or any of the professions or trades— a Christian understanding of life and work recognizes that authentic engagement with our world is one that is *thoughtful*: that is, we cultivate the life of the mind. This suggests to us two things. First, on the one hand it means we take our own minds seriously—we appreciate that the intellectual life is not left to scholars but that all of us are called to approach life and work, and particularly our specific callings, in a manner that is truthful—informed and anchored within the Christian intellectual tradition. And second, this means that we value and appreciate our scholars, teachers, writers, and those whose calling it is to foster our thoughtful engagement with life and work.

The Christian religious and spiritual tradition, building on its Judeo-Christian heritage, affirms this kind of work and recognizes its critical importance for religious communities and for society. One of the marks of authentic Christian faith and community is that we call for intellectual rigor in our pursuit of what it means to be human and to be Christian.[1] Gerard W. Hughes, in his book *God of Surprises*, states this very well:

> A mark of true Christianity will be its intellectual vigor and its search for meaning in every aspect of life. . . . That is why there has been such an emphasis on scholarship and learning in the Christian tradition.[2]

And as such we need to celebrate and affirm the work of the scholar—the calling to and the cultivation of the life of the mind: the work of nurturing critical understanding, discerning perception, and appreciating new discoveries or ways of seeing and engaging reality—the reality of God's world. The life of the mind is fundamental to what it means to be Christian—to mature in faith, hope, and love, and to grow in our capacity for wisdom. And for all of us, the contribution of our scholars is fundamental: they are gifts of God to the church and to the world.

I am not saying they are more important than plumbers or nurses. That is why this chapter needs the one that follows (on the work of our hands). But nevertheless, we need to stress that this work—scholarship and the cultivation of the life of the mind—is of utmost importance to both the church and society and that as such it needs to be profiled and encouraged. We need to lean into those who nurture the life of the mind for the church and for the world. Without those who help us foster thoughtfulness—scholars and teachers—we are lost. All of us need them to cultivate our capacity to think clearly and deeply, to discern well, and to grow in wisdom. That is the bottom line: not merely good work, not merely being present to the here and now, not merely discerning our vocation, but most fundamentally that we are growing in wisdom.

Christian thinking applies to not only scholars or academics but to each Christian, regardless of their life circumstances or their vocation. Our approach to life and work is always shaped by some vision of reality, some understanding or perspective that is informing our approach to the relationships, vocation, or career we have. It is either Christian or it is secular; in other words, the Christian mind refuses to compartmentalize and assume that "Christian" refers to religious. Rather a Christian mind refers to how we think about every aspect of life and work—whether our faith and religious practices or our approach to banking, to buying and selling, to matters of legality and morality. Harry Blamires, years ago, made this distinction between Christian thinking and secular thinking and then, naturally, stressed that we need to learn to think Christianly about all of life and all of our ways of engaging the world through our work. But then he rightly and aptly notes that we can also think in a secular way about religious life and practice. We can approach worship and liturgy and everything from how we govern the church to how the church seeks to grow and propagate its message in a *secular* manner. And thus his point: we are secular until and unless we learn what it means to think Christianly about all of life—our religious practices and our work in the world.[3]

THE HALLMARKS OF THE CHRISTIAN MIND

What do we mean by "a Christian mind"? If we are going to talk about thinking Christianly, it only follows that we need to be able to give some kind of answer to this question. While there are many different ways in which this could be framed, at the very least a Christian mind is marked by six distinctive features or hallmarks—ways of being, seeing, and thinking—which I offer here as a way to promote conversation about what we mean by cultivating and encouraging a thoughtful way of fostering Christian identity. Consider six words that give us a window into what we mean by a Christian mind: transcendence, truth, reason, sin, love, and wisdom.

Transcendence. A Christian mind cultivates an intentional awareness that what is real and what is true includes much more than what we can see, taste, and touch. We share this perspective with all religious traditions, of course: an awareness of another sphere of reality beyond the material world. For the Christian, we specifically affirm that transcendence speaks of a triune and personal God—Father, Son, and Spirit—known to us through the revelation of God's self in Scripture, the God who has created all things and is redeeming all things. From this perspective, a Christian mind leads us to worship.

Truth. A Christian mind cultivates a love for truth and a commitment to name reality, to know the truth, and then, of course, to live in a way that is consistent with the truth because truth is foundational to human flourishing. While all truth is God's truth, the heart or centerpiece of truth is found through God's self-revelation, in creation

74

but then centrally and specifically in Scripture. Thus, Christians consistently read, proclaim, and live by the Word. From this perspective, a Christian mind leads to obedience—deference to the truth.

Sin. The Christian mind is one that recognizes all things have been created by God and that there is a fundamental goodness to creation—the physical, tangible world in which we live, including our own embodiment. But also, the Christian mind knows there was a "fall"—something went awry. It is called sin. And we call sin *sin*; we use the *s* word to speak of the fragmentation of the created order and the reality that things are not as they were or are meant to be. We do not make light of the human predicament. And, of course, taken together with transcendence, there is the realization that the only hope for a fragmented world and the healing of creation is divine intervention. From this perspective, a Christian mind leads to humility, repentance, and dependence on the grace of God.

Reason (and discernment). A Christian mind cultivates a commitment to clear, logical, and rational thinking, exemplified by the articulation of the gospel—of truth—as found in Paul's epistle to the Romans. A Christian mind is reasonable and is resolved to foster the capacity to discern what is good, noble, and excellent. From this perspective, a Christian mind leads to informed decisions and behavior. We do not polarize head and heart, affect and emotion, but we weigh decisions in a manner that is thoughtful, informed by careful reasoning and clear-minded deliberation.

Love. A Christian mind cultivates an appreciation that truth and understanding are not ends in themselves but means by which we can live lives of generosity for our neighbor. From this perspective, a Christian mind leads to service—a life lived for God and for the world.

Wisdom. A Christian mind leans into instruction and education and learning, such that Christians value highly the role of the teacher who is able to foster growth in knowledge, which leads to growth in wisdom. From this perspective, then, the Christian mind is teachable.

We do our work, then, with a vision of life and our world that is marked by a powerful transcendence: that all of life is infused by an awareness of the God who has created all things and is redeeming all things, and that truth and reason and wisdom call us to our best selves and to a vision of human flourishing that finds expression in generous love for our neighbor.

> **THE CHRISTIAN MIND IS TEACHABLE.**

What all of this presumes, though, is a disposition of the heart. Fear and anger undercut our capacity to cultivate a Christian mind. Understanding comes not merely through rational argument, but through the cultivation of faith and openness to the truth. For the Christian, we can speak of "faith seeking understanding." We cannot assume that we can argue someone into the faith merely through persuasive logic. All understanding and growth in wisdom is located within a person and a community that has a heart and inner disposition of openness, attentiveness, and willingness to know God and to live in the truth.

THREATS TO THE CHRISTIAN MIND

This vital part of our lives—tending to the life of the mind—is under threat. There is a powerful strain of anti-intellectualism in both the church and in society at large. I am not going to be so melodramatic as to say it is under threat like never before; that might be an overstatement. But it is under threat in at least three ways where we can see thoughtfulness is being discounted and undervalued—ironically or tragically, when it is most critically needed.

I am going to speak to pragmatism, sentimentalism, and partisan propaganda. All three in some form or another discount, if not actually undercut, the vital place of the work and contribution of the scholar.

By *pragmatism*, I mean the reduction of the life of the mind to a narrow outcome—a job or career.[4] The only reason for thinking or study, the only reason for an education, is that we get a job. And thus, the only value in any reading or study we might do is to enhance our capacity or skills to deliver certain outcomes. Sociologists speak of this as "credentialing": that study and education and learning is about being "trained," having the skills to get a job done. Students, and often their parents who reinforce this, are so concerned with their careers. They come out of high school obsessed with getting a job—a well-paying career with the potential for promotions and ultimately financial security. For them, a university is not so much a place for growing in wisdom with the capacity to think critically and write well and cultivate character and moral intelligence, but rather a way to get a powerful résumé that will land a "great" job.

Few have spoken so aptly to this trend as Martha C. Nussbaum. See, in particular, her *Not for Profit: Why Democracy Needs the Humanities*, where her focus is government expectations of colleges and universities, but what she has to say is equally applicable to church denominations that have a similar propensity.[5] She tackles the ways in which governments focus entirely on education as a means for economic gain that discounts the need to foster the capacity to think critically and creatively. These capacities are often cultivated through the humanities and thus these disciplines—history, English, philosophy—are viewed as less than economically helpful.

I am not for a moment questioning the need for skills or competency or for being credentialed for a profession or for leadership in the church. All universities should be vibrant communities where good work is celebrated and students are equipped to discern their vocations and enter into a lifetime of fruitful service, both in the church and in society. And yes, of course, the society and the church need competent and capable university graduates.

> WE FAIL OUR YOUNG PEOPLE IF WE DO NOT EQUALLY GIVE THEM THE SKILLS TO THINK CRITICALLY AND IMAGINATIVELY AND TO CULTIVATE EMOTIONAL AND MORAL INTELLIGENCE.

Rather, the concern is twofold: that we have too narrow a definition of what we mean by skills for the economy or for the church and, second, that we fail our young people if we do not equally give them the skills to think critically and imaginatively and, along the way, cultivate emotional and moral intelligence. The bottom line is ultimately that we grow in wisdom.

Second, *sentimentalism*. I am not sure if there is a better word for this, but what I mean to highlight is the craving for experience that bypasses critical intellectual engagement—depth of emotion without a corresponding engagement of the mind.[6] Jonathan Edwards, perhaps the greatest of all American theologians, spoke of this as spiritually dangerous, stressing that all true religious affections are informed by clarity of understanding. The genius of his British counterpart, John Wesley, was the integration of heart and mind. There is a proclivity, whether in the church or in society at large, to pursue experience—heightened religious experience—without reference to critical thought. We see this in the desire for preachers and speakers for our churches or our church conferences or assemblies who are more likely to be revivalists than thoughtful expositors. There is a longing for inspiration through exciting stories and a failure to see that, without engaging the mind, the sentiments are fleeting and superficial: depth of affection requires—back to Jonathan Edwards—depth of thought.

This does not mean that emotion does not matter. Of course not. The genius of the Christian spiritual tradition is that we can speak of the integration of head and heart, intellect and affect. We can affirm the place of emotion in human experience. Rather, sentimentalism is the propensity to discount the importance of the life of the mind as something integral to any genuine experience.

> THE GENIUS OF THE
> CHRISTIAN SPIRITUAL
> TRADITION IS THAT
> WE CAN SPEAK OF
> THE INTEGRATION
> OF HEAD AND
> HEART, INTELLECT
> AND AFFECT.

And then third, we need to also consider that which we might speak of as *partisan propaganda*: that engagement of the mind that is only and purely one of reinforcing what we already know or want to know or believe, with the refusal to see another perspective or even want to know and face the truth. Joel Thiessen speaks of "partisan reductionism" and defines it as

a set of ideas or beliefs, often economic or political in nature, that serve as the rather simple, one or two variable, all-encompassing theoretical prism by which one sees, analyzes, and behaves in the world, almost to the exclusion—or worse, shaming—of other more complex, nuanced, and even competing frameworks. Those who hold this approach also tend to refute the possibility that they could be wrong.[7]

By partisan propaganda, I mean the use of data or information solely for a political or ideological agenda. Media and journalism then become a means for disseminating an ideological agenda rather than fostering true understanding. Church teaching is all about indoctrination—making sure young people hold the same theological views as their parents' generation. Opposing views are demonized; critical thought and thus discussion are viewed as a threat to the views of those in authority—whether in the civic square or in denominational leadership. The critical value is compliance—whether in the political realm or within the church: unquestioned deference to authority. Hard questions—and true journalism—are a threat, of course, and thus authoritarian regimes do all they can to marginalize the free press. And within the church, we *shush* those who might be playing a similar role—viewing hard questions or any kind of dissent as an indicator that a person is not a genuine team player or sufficiently loyal to the denomination.

I am not for a moment suggesting we do not affirm a theological and intellectual heritage in the church—that is, that we do not position ourselves within a particular tradition, whether that be Mennonite or Calvinian or Wesleyan or Catholic or Orthodox. Nor am I saying that those of a particular ideological persuasion cannot or should not make a case for their views. Not at all. What needs to be challenged is, rather, the polarizing dismissal of critical discussion and views that might challenge the prevailing assumptions of our particular tribe.

Perhaps there are more, but at the very least, pragmatism, sentimentalism, and partisan propaganda are three threats to the Christian mind. And all three are current threats to the life and work of the church and to schools and to universities and to society at large. And the challenge of our responses is complicated by two things. First, to use the phrase coined by W. H. Auden, we live in an "age of anxiety." Our fear keeps us from thinking critically and carefully. Second, we are distracted, with hardly the attention span needed to have a deep thought.

CULTIVATING CRITICAL, CONFIDENT, CREATIVE, AND COMPASSIONATE THINKING

Given the threats, and given our anxious and distracted age, we need to be intentional. To that end, I suggest the following: Our capacity for thoughtful engagement with life and work, informed by the Christian intellectual and spiritual tradition, would mean that we take care of the life of the mind. We see "mind care" as fundamental to our spiritual health and well-being. To reference the common language of "soul care," we must insist that there is no soul care without care for the mind. There is no spiritual growth and maturity without intellectual engagement.

One way to think of this is to intentionally pursue the capacity for critical, confident, creative, and compassionate thinking.

By *critical*, we do not mean being judgmental but rather the capacity to see clearly and with discernment and not be swayed by appeals that are nothing more than emotional manipulation. We can see past the hype. We can assess an argument or the case being made. We can weigh the merits of a position being espoused and see if the view or position makes sense. We can hear a sermon or a lecture or read an editorial or an opinion piece and recognize thoughtfulness and careful reasoning. We can be open-minded and eager to learn, but also refuse to be gullible. We can challenge our own biases and prejudices. We have no patience with hype or mere sentimentality. We can follow social media but do so in a way that does not simply reinforce what we already want to believe.

By *confident* thinking, I mean the capacity to speak and think for oneself—to be able to come to one's own conclusions and think, not so much independently but interdependently.

Yes, we are in conversation with others, and we are accountable to others in our thinking, and we are willing and able to be challenged regarding our views and perspectives. However, the key here is that even though we lean into the wisdom of others, we are able to voice an opinion and engage the conversation while remaining humble enough to change our minds. And, in the meantime and along the way, we can speak for ourselves—and our views and our opinions are very much our views and our opinions, and we are more than prepared to speak to them.

By *creative*, I mean a mind—a way of thinking—that is capable of innovation and adaptability: that is, a mind that has an active imagination. This dimension of a Christian mind is one that, as often as not, is nurtured by fiction, poetry, drama, music, and the visual arts. The artists in our midst are as crucial to the cultivation of a Christian mind as any scholar or intellectual leader; thoughtful Christians move comfortably from the library to the art museum, from an evening with their book club debating about a new publication on social policy to an evening with friends attending a performance of the local string quartet.

And by *compassionate*, we mean the capacity for empathy. Compassionate thinking is decentered thinking—meaning we step outside of our own situation or perspective and see the world, especially those less fortunate, through the lens of their experiences. We ask with an open heart and mind what it means to experience our situation, our society, our church, our educational system through the eyes and experience of another of a different race, ethnicity, and background.

For each of these—critical, confident, creative, and compassionate—being intentional in our cultivation of the life of the mind fosters our capacity to resist, or not succumb to, the threats of pragmatism, sentimentalism, and partisan propaganda.

READING AND THE LIFE OF THE MIND

Naturally, we then ask, If we take the life of the mind seriously and value the work of scholars and intellectual leaders, how do we lean into and allow their work to inform our lives and our work? On this score, there is little debate: we cultivate the life of the mind through good teaching and good conversation informed by and fueled by the quality—the depth and breadth—of our reading. If we take the life of the mind seriously, it will be evident in the books we choose to read. It means we are fans of libraries and bookstores, and that we take time and space to read. And it means that we choose to read widely, tending to thought leaders who do not merely reinforce what we already know or believe but challenge us and deepen our thinking.

> CHOOSE TO READ WIDELY, TENDING TO THOUGHT LEADERS WHO DO NOT MERELY REINFORCE WHAT WE ALREADY KNOW OR BELIEVE BUT CHALLENGE US AND DEEPEN OUR THINKING.

We read newer publications, but we also read older books. In his delightful introduction to an ancient book, *Saint Athanasius on the Incarnation*, C. S. Lewis makes an appeal: that yes, while of course we read new books and new publications that reflect some of the best thinking of our generation, we should surely also be reading older books. He notes it is often assumed only students of history would read older books. And yet, as he observes, older books have stood the test of time and they anchor us in the ancient conversation about the faith and the implications of the faith—that is, wisdom—for living and working well. And his rule of thumb with regard to the books one reads is that we should ideally "never allow yourself another new one till you have read an old one in between."[8]

As a Christian, perhaps start with the *Confessions* of Saint Augustine, but then also you might discover an ancient voice from the early church that becomes for you a regular source of wisdom and encouragement. Then also, do not be shy about reading voices from the Middle Ages—not at all the so-called "dark" ages, but rather sources of profound wisdom on prayer and the spiritual life. I am personally deeply indebted to A. W. Tozer, who in 1963 published his remarkable collection titled *The Christian Book of Mystical Verse: A Collection of Poems, Hymns, and Prayers for Devotional Reading* that opened me up to an extensive body of literature I had previously known nothing about.[9] And then a few years later, still in my late twenties, I took a course from James Houston at Regent College on the history of Christian spirituality that covered the landscape from the early to the contemporary church and critical voices in between. With Tozer and Houston as my original guides, I now value and lean into the wisdom of the eleventh and sixteenth and seventeenth centuries as much as any other source of reading that shapes my thinking: Saint John of the Cross, Teresa of Avila,

Ignatius Loyola, along with, of course, John Calvin and Martin Luther.

Read older books, but also read history. Get to know historians, who provide an essential context—the story behind the story—for much of what is happening in the world today. Read social commentary and political analysis. Read on faith and belief and doctrine. Join a book club and meet monthly to discuss a book you have each read, and listen and engage in thoughtful, challenging conversation about the significance of the book that has been your focus for the last month. Read history and social commentary and theology and spirituality together. But then also read fiction. Fiction plays a key role in cultivating our capacity for compassionate thinking; we are placed within the experience of another and see the world—the joys and sorrows of life and work—through the eyes of another; our field of vision and experience is broadened. And lest I lose all my food-loving friends, yes, you must read a cookbook or two!

IN READING BOOKS FROM OTHER CULTURES AND OTHER RELIGIOUS COMMUNITIES, WE HAVE A BETTER UNDERSTANDING OF OUR WORLD; THEY CHALLENGE OUR WORLDVIEW.

Read voices that emerge from the Global South and from religious traditions other than your own. What we often find is that in reading books coming from other cultures and other religious communities, we have a better understanding of our world; they challenge our worldview. And often, I find voices from other religious communities highlight something that, while profoundly Christian, my own religious community has perhaps neglected to affirm. I think here of how many Christians have valued the insights and perspectives of Thich Nhat Hanh, Vietnamese Buddhist monk, especially his call to mindfulness, and in the upcoming chapter I am going to reference Matthew Crawford who calls all of us, Christians included, to a greater appreciation of the work of our hands.

Read poetry—get to know some of the best of older poets and some contemporary poets who ably capture your imagination and help you make sense of what is happening to you both intellectually and emotionally. And have a podcast—or two—that you turn to regularly as a source of both insight and encouragement. It is perhaps important to mention that much of our reading will take place digitally—online, on a screen. There is no doubt there is huge value in using online resources; the array of voices in the digital world might not otherwise be accessible to us. But increasingly, we are seeing what is aptly called "deep reading," which highlights how leisured, careful, and ultimately transformative reading needs to include the hard copy text in our hands as our brains engage the digital world differently from the printed text.[10]

Finally, whatever our vocation or calling, read the thought leaders within your field—exploring what it means to think theologically about your work: whether in banking and finance, or in medicine and nursing, or in business and the world of commerce. The word *theology* should not be viewed as elitist or purely academic; rather, we ask, what are the resources—the intellectual leaders—who will help me think about my work and my vocation through the lens of the Christian vision of the work of God in the world. I will seek to think Christianly about my work. If I am an artist or a businessperson or a schoolteacher or a civic leader, I will very intentionally be reading those whose work can shape my capacity to do my work with theological integrity. Look for the best insights into the meaning of your work—the theology of business or medicine or law. Artists find valued sources to help them think about the meaning of their work as painters, actors, and musicians.

And then of course, this is why effective pastors need to be judged in part by the quality of their libraries. When I visit a pastor in their office and they step out to get us both a cup of coffee, I take the opportunity to glance over their libraries and see who they are reading—who shapes their vision for life, work, and ministry, and informs their preaching and approaches to pastoral care and missional engagement. Are they reading critical exegetical studies as well as guides to the meaning of secularity and the challenge of race relations? Are they reading fiction and poetry and everything from environmental studies to the history of baseball to a biography of Beethoven? They may not be scholars; that is not their calling. But are they leaning into and depending on the work of scholars? And I mention pastors in particular in that inevitably they set an example for all of us: Is their ministry to us thoughtful and do they challenge members of their congregations to read widely and deeply and approach life and work in a way that is theologically informed?[11]

CONCLUSION

So, where does all of this leave us? If we are going to be fully present to our here and now, to recognize and respond to the call of God for this time and this place, it will be in large measure because we have learned what it means to approach life and work thoughtfully. And yet, the bottom line is not ultimately about thoughtful work, but about the call of God to grow in wisdom. That is, we do all this reading to this end: the call of Proverbs 4—that, whatever else we get, we get wisdom (Prov 4:7). That, through the journey of life, work, and career, we hold on to instruction (Prov 4:13) and grow in knowledge and insight, and as such, the older we get, may it be so, the wiser we become.

QUESTIONS FOR REFLECTION AND DISCUSSION

1. In your current social and religious context, what is the greatest threat to the life of the mind? Is it pragmatism, sentimentalism, or partisan propaganda?

2. For your own reading, what comes to mind as a topic—theology, fiction, history perhaps?—or an author that you have been intending to read and recognize you need to make a priority to find the time to take up that book or resource?

6

THE WORK OF OUR HANDS

You HAVE PERHAPS SEEN those bumper stickers with some variation of the message, "My other car is . . ." They are likely driving what in my part of the world we call a "beater," but the sticker speaks of a supposed high-end sports car, such as, "My other car is a Lamborghini." If I were to have such a sticker on the back bumper of my car, it would be: "My other car is a 1998 Toyota Tacoma." And in my case, it is quite literally my other car. I know, that may not strike those who read the bumper sticker as having much cachet. But I quite like this smaller, older pickup truck and happily drive it any chance I get. Notable is that this delightful machine has a five-speed on-the-floor manual transmission. And part of why I enjoy driving my '98 Tacoma is not merely that it is very practical—useful for carting all manner of things—but also precisely because it has a *manual* transmission.

There is something visceral in listening to and feeling the work of the engine and kicking in the gear changes to bring it up to speed and then gearing down for the upcoming curve in the road. I like the feel—yes, that is the word—of driving with a manual transmission, which for me at least, means I have a higher level of connection with the vehicle and the road. This is not the kind of truck or car you want to drive on an express way or through heavy rush-hour bumper-to-bumper traffic with constant start and stop. In those situations, you no doubt want an automatic transmission. But on back roads—on gentle two-lane highways through the hill country—this is a dream machine precisely because it has a manual transmission.

It is that manual side of things that will be explored here: to consider what it means to work with our hands for all of us and then, in particular, for those for whom this is their daily work or vocation. That is, consider what it means to celebrate those for whom their work is *manual* labor; their vocation is that of working with their hands. And, along the way, to consider what the work of our hands means to all of us.

Doing this requires that we affirm the dignity and worth of such work—that is, that we view this kind of work to have the potential to be sacred and called of God. But here is our challenge: For so many of us, our deep sensibilities have been formed by cultural mores that discount or discredit manual work. We see this from both East and West, notably by cultures that have been shaped by Confucianism in the East or by the Greek or Hellenistic world in the West. Confucian scholars were known to grow their fingernails long as a way of making it abundantly clear they did not do physical labor. In the Confucian system of social ranking, artisans and those who worked with their hands were at the bottom—least valued or respected. In societies and cultures that have had significant influence from Confucian thought, it is commonly assumed that you are successful in life and work and career if you and your children move up and onward from working with your hands. It is not uncommon that it is viewed as shameful to do physical labor, especially farming, and so one aspired that one's children would move into the professions such as law, medicine, and engineering.

For those from Western societies influenced by Greek or Hellenistic philosophy, there is a similar undercurrent when it comes to thinking and talking about work. There is not only a dichotomy between mental and manual work, but also an implicit assumption in our language—that there are classes of people who are "laborers," that there is a distinction between white-collar and blue-collar work, and that there is more pride and prestige and honor to have a job in the "professions" rather than in the "trades." As with those from the East, one would rather a daughter was a lawyer than a seamstress or carpenter or plumber or electrician. That is, in both the East and West, many are part of religious subcultures that disparage manual work—the calling into the trades, and other forms of manual work that are indispensable to human life. We equate "manual" with "menial."

In contrast, the Judeo-Christian religious and spiritual tradition is marked by a high affirmation and celebration of the practical arts—the work of the artisan, the craftsperson, the farmer, the work of our hands. It is interesting that even the created order is spoken of as the *handiwork* of God (Ps 19:1), thus celebrating God as a manual worker, we might say, so much so that if God works with his hands, why would we not celebrate the work of our hands? And this is precisely what we see in Proverbs 31 where the wise woman who is profiled as the summation and pinnacle of the book of Proverbs is described again and again with reference to her hands. Much as the hands and handiwork of God are celebrated, she is not only a businesswoman, buying and selling land and products, she is also described as one who works with willing hands (Prov 31:13). Her hands are found on the distaff and the spindle, and she makes things—she clothes her family with the fruit of the work of her hands (Prov 31:19, 22). Thus, the grand finale of this section of Proverbs, and indeed the last verse of this book of the Bible, is a call to "give her a share in the fruit of her hands," and to let her work be celebrated and affirmed in the city. Also not to be missed is that her hands are referenced with regard to her generosity to the poor (Prov 31:20).

What all of this suggests to us is that it is imperative—essential and life-affirming—to recognize the significance of this work: to see it as intimately associated with the work of God, and as therefore having dignity and worth. And this means two things. First, that we affirm and celebrate those for whom manual work is the essence or at the heart of their calling. And second, that we all learn to work with our hands and see handiwork as not merely something that is done for us but something we learn to do: we are comfortable in the kitchen, the carpentry shop, the quilting studio.

> **WE AFFIRM AND CELEBRATE THOSE FOR WHOM MANUAL WORK IS THE ESSENCE OR AT THE HEART OF THEIR CALLING.**

We can make things, fix things, tend to the practical details of our lives with both skill and joy. We can affirm the work and vocation of those for whom this is their daily work, and we can come to see how our own work, with our hands, is an essential means by which we fulfill our human calling or vocation—for none of us is manual work "beneath" us. We come to see that such a way of thinking is actually ungodly.

THE WORK OF THE CRAFTSPERSON

Daily—literally daily—we live in multiple forms of dependence on the work of those for whom manual labor is their livelihood: whether farmers or those in the various trades associated with the construction of houses or those who make our clothing and tend to the roads and pathways and sidewalks that make our cities accessible and livable. Life does not happen and could not happen without the practical skills and commitment of those who work with their hands. They are indispensable to what it means to be human. Because their work is so indispensable, it only makes sense that we would affirm and celebrate the work of skilled, creative, and thoughtful practitioners of these trades—so that the plumbing in our homes works, so that the food on our table is organic and nutritious, and so the vehicle we are driving runs smoothly. It is simply naive and presumptuous that those Confucian scholars would think this kind of work is beneath them: they want to eat well and have a roof over their heads. No doubt. So why would we not within our common lives, rather than grudgingly accept their work as somehow minimally necessary, instead actually affirm, celebrate, and appropriately compensate them for their work?

Compensation is a way we typically signal that this work matters. And yet, we somehow resist giving them their due. Yes, of late those in the trades have been able—and rightly— to secure better remuneration. But the perception is that we are willing to pay a lawyer much more than we would pay a plumber or an electrician. But why? What is the basis for this supposed hierarchy of skills or vocations within our society? I need both the physician that provides me with a good diagnosis, and I need the farmer who works to put food on my table. We need the facilities manager who installs the doors and tends to the lighting of the university classroom and the professor who teaches in that space. Both need the other: and thus, the oh-so-apt line from the apostle Paul: "The eye cannot say to the hand, 'I have no need of you,' nor again the head to the feet, 'I have no need of you,'" (1 Cor 12:21). Paul goes on to stress that we must not clothe with lesser honor those seemingly less "respectable" roles. While he is speaking in this epistle to the life of the church, the principle applies to what it means to be a society that hopefully learns to truly appreciate those whose work— while being manual—is not menial.

The point in all of this is that we need to resist the idea that good and faithful parents are always and necessarily encouraging their children to go into the so-called "professions." Why cannot the son of a physician choose to be a carpenter and find this work to be deeply gratifying? Why do we persist within our social networks to be more impressed when someone tells us their daughter has become a lawyer rather than if they told us she had chosen to be a small plot farmer producing food for an organic grocer?

Why do we think those who build our houses are of less worth or significance than the architect who designs the house? Why not within our communities find ways to affirm, recognize, and celebrate those whose work is so deeply practical, and do so in a way that encourages young people to genuinely consider callings or vocations that might fall under the rubric of "manual"?

But here also, we can and must speak to the artisan—the potter, the fine carpenter who crafts the one-off chair out of driftwood, the cook in his kitchen with no pretensions of being a chef but delights in the preparation of quality meals beautifully presented. If the carpenter builds the bed, that work is complemented by the quilter who works to create the beauty that adorns that bed. As I write this, I do so at an exquisitely designed desk—a piece of beautiful furniture that is a reminder to me of the line attributed to William Morris: "Have nothing in your house that you do not know to be useful, or believe to be beautiful." This desk is both so very useful and also clearly something that is beautifully crafted. It is the artisans who through their craft enrich our lives—whether with pottery, quilts, a knitted cap or scarf, or a piece of furniture that a trained eye recognizes to be the work of a master.

WORKING WITH OUR HANDS

We need to learn what it means to affirm and celebrate and value the work of those whose work and trade provides for our very practical needs. But we can and need to go further and reflect on the work of our *own* hands. Matthew Crawford reminds his readers that the best of the Western tradition, going back to Homer, is the appreciation that to be wise is to be skilled and, more precisely, to be skilled at a craft.[1] And that it was only in more recent centuries that wisdom has come to be linked merely with knowledge and the intellectual life. Might we not then conclude that wise women and men are informed and knowledgeable and *also* capable of working with their hands?

Could it be that Proverbs 31 is making this very point? This chapter is a culmination of the entire book of Proverbs—a kind of capstone. Might it be that in all that has been said about wisdom from Proverbs 1 through 30—the call to wisdom along with warnings and encouragements and aphorisms and sayings—we come to this final chapter, and it has

> WISE WOMEN AND MEN ARE INFORMED AND KNOWLEDGEABLE AND *ALSO* CAPABLE OF WORKING WITH THEIR HANDS.

described for us what it means to be a person of wisdom, and that it is a person who works with willing hands? Wisdom is found, of course, through knowledge and understanding, and a life well lived with constraint in speech, sexuality, and finances—recurring themes in the book of Proverbs. But what is interesting—intentional and thus not incidental—is that the wise woman of Proverbs 31 is someone who is adept with her hands. Manual work, it seems, is a sign of wisdom.

In other words, perhaps we only truly appreciate the work of those whose primary work or occupation is manual when we *ourselves*, each one of us, learn—at least minimally—to work with *our* hands: to delight in the garden—whether it is in planting or harvesting or pruning or watering—or find enjoyment in a workshop or in repairing machines or renovating a home. That is, that regardless of our day job, we know what it is on the weekend to choose to spend a day in a workshop rather than on a golf course, tending some craft, building a birdhouse or a kayak. Perhaps we join the quilters guild—amateurs in the sense that it is for the love of this work and not specifically for compensation as a wage earner.

Speaking of the amateur is not to discount or minimize the work of those who do their work as a source of their livelihood. We need them and value them; some have the capacity to repair their own furnace on a cold winter night or have the mechanical know-how to rebuild an engine or resole a shoe. Some may have the capacity to source all their own food. We all—literally, all of us—depend on some manual expertise of others. And yet, surely on some level we should not be so dependent that we have no capacity or ability or desire to work with our own hands and be good at what we do: whether it is basic maintenance of our homes or the pottery wheel in the basement or the motorcycle we are rebuilding in the back shed.

What is interesting is to look back to the ancient Rule of Saint Benedict that governed the lives of the ancient monastic communities. Chapter 48 of the Rule specifies that manual work is the essential complement to other dimensions of the life of the monks, notably study and prayer.[2] And with Benedict, you get the sense that manual work does two things. First, it grounds us; we are living not merely in our heads, but in our bodies. We are connected to our bodies, to the earth, to the materiality all around us.

And second, it dignifies us. Manual work does not demean us; to the contrary, the Scriptures and our Christian heritage affirm how manual work dignifies the human person and the human community. And this means, of course, that not only is this kind of work not beneath us, but we can also go further and appreciate that the work we do with our hands is *ennobling*. It can be a source of significant joy—the delight that comes in spreading out the ingredients on the kitchen counter and then, with the right knife in hand, bringing together the stir fry that will be the central dish for a meal. Or the joy that comes with stepping back after you have put the finishing touches on a piece of furniture or repaired the brakes on your car or built a birdhouse and then within the day have tree swallows move in and start making a nest. Sometimes it is hard slogging, no doubt; sometimes you just want to throw up your hands and order take-out and eat off a paper plate in front of the television. Sometimes the task at hand is too much and you need to call in an expert. But there is nothing quite like the joy of having done it yourself—you've created something useful or beautiful or, ideally, both.

As noted, working with our hands is a source of joy, but it is also a means of grace to us. It is exalting; rather than a source of shame or degradation, manual work actually dignifies. It is a supremely Godlike act or way of being. Like God—not presuming to be God, but rather living out what it means to be created in the image of God—we too can do precisely what God has done and is doing: work with our hands and then step back and delight in that work. We can recognize that it is good. We can without hesitation consider what we have made and delight in the birdhouse we have put together or the garden we have planted or the quilt we just completed.

But there is more. We are embodied souls; there is a very real sense in which our souls are only truly animated—alive, connected—when they are not in disconnect mode but fully present to and in this body. We speak of the integration of head and heart, of the ideal where critical intellectual reflection is matched by and fueled by the ordering of our affections. We long for the ideal of head and heart mutually informing the other. But could it be that this only can happen if we are thoroughly embodied? Thus, the Eucharist or Lord's Supper as a supremely tangible and bodily activity of worship is the essential counterpart to the hearty singing and the thoughtful sermon. The Lord's Table grounds us; for, indeed, if our understanding and the movement of our hearts is not ultimately embodied, it is not an overstatement to say that it never actually takes. It has to be grounded; we are only women and men of faith when that faith is not merely cerebral or sentimental but actually infused into the marrow of our bones. It happens in the body, or it does not happen at all.

And when we work with our hands—like other embodied actions, including the Lord's Supper and meals together and walking as spiritual practice—we are doing things in and with our bodies, with our hands, that ground our souls: they connect head and heart. In other words, they make us truly human. Just as we know God as truly God by virtue of the work of God's hands, in like manner, our humanity is not disembodied: we are truly human in part because we work with our hands.

And so, one of the gifts we can give to children is toys that require them to manipulate this or that or the other—to build things, to enjoy making things with paper or building blocks or, the high point of all child activities, to build a sandcastle on the beach. It does not take much; joy comes easily when we are building things. But then we can get beyond play and actually invite children to join us in our manual tasks around the house—whether in meal preparation or raking leaves or planting the garden or putting together a birdhouse. As parents and grandparents, we can invite them to come alongside and experience the joy of working with their hands and knowing the satisfaction of a job well done. I am reminded of the joy of a granddaughter working with me on a particular challenge, and when we did it, her sheer delight, "We did it, Grandpa!" And we encourage teens, regardless of their ultimate vocational aspirations, to find a summer job that has them working with their hands and developing a skill or two that could be useful to them along the way. Who knows, they might in so doing discover their own sense of call. But the main benefit is that whatever their calling, they will have a greater appreciation for those for whom this is their occupation, their livelihood, their vocation. And they will be increasingly comfortable with the work of their own hands.

THE TOOLS OF THE CRAFT

Every vocation or occupation has its tools—the tools of the craft: the physician's stethoscope, the chef's knives, the writer's pen, the artist's brush, the weaver's loom, the watch-repairer's eye loupe. What they consistently find is that if they take their work seriously—whatever the vocation, but now specifically to speak about those for whom their vocation is "the work of their hands"—that tools, well-designed, ergonomically beautiful tools, are so vital and central to their capacity to do their work and do it well. Those who work with their hands have a high affinity and respect for these instruments of their work: whether the tractor with its powerful backhoe or the hickory-handled hammer that is beautifully crafted and weighted perfectly, whether power tools or the simple yet essential garden shovel. From the loom to the kitchen knives to the rake, those who work with their hands are very particular about their tools. In my part of the world, it is fun to visit a store known as Lee Valley and just stroll the aisles but also listen to the women and men who are the serious buyers as they consider what quality tool will do the job for them. Those who work with their hands, whether professional or amateur, prize their tools as vital and essential to their work.

But still, it is *manual* work; it is the work of our hands. In his delightful memoir on his work as a carpenter, Ole Thorstensen speaks about every aspect of trade—from the business side of things as he wrestles with the finances of being an independent contractor, to the comradery he has with others in the trades, to both his joys and frustrations in working on an awkward and challenging house renovation. But what is not to be missed is the way he speaks about his own hands. Yes, of course, his work requires a huge inventory of quality tools. And yet, he writes:

> I like my hands; they have been formed by my age and
> my work. Some scars, none of them large, all fingers

intact, they are my work: carpenter's hands. The skin is hard, yet free of calluses; it is a long time since I have had them. The skin on them is like a thick work glove. My history can be read in them, I think; my hands look like what I have done and so in life. They are a testimonial, my personal CV.[3]

And later he speaks of them as tools: "My hands are tools in direct contact with the materials and whatever else I work with. When pulling up a floor I wear gloves, but I prefer working with my bare hands when carrying out ordinary carpentry."[4]

For certain, gardeners know that when you are pruning a rose bush, you do not want one of those thorns in your thumb! But any chance they have to work with the direct feel of their work on their hands, they'll doff the gloves and feel the wood, the soil, the clay, or the fabric.

PRAYER AND THE WORK OF OUR HANDS

Many for whom their primary work is with their hands are also those who have a pattern or rhythm to their days and their work, where their work—and routines and practices, often repetitive—is complemented by intercessory prayer. And why not? Manual work is thoughtful: one has to be creative, inventive, and attentive to the work that one has in hand, whether in the kitchen or the workshop or the garden. And yet, manual work also gives one time and space to think; it can often be done in a way that is not all consuming. Perhaps that is part of its beauty. While working with a colleague installing a deck outside a home, you can be chatting along the way about the kids and church politics and the news of the day.

And this means that when working alone, manual work is so frequently an ideal time for tending to our prayers. We are still attentive to what we are doing—fully present. And yet, at the same time, especially if it has a rhythm or repetitive nature to it—planting the seeds in spring for the substantial garden, sanding and re-sanding the piece of furniture, working stone by stone to create the garden wall—one has the freedom to attend with heart and mind to those concerns that percolate to the surface of our minds.

To pray for our children and grandchildren, our nieces and nephews, as we go through the chores of the day. To think of and pray for our neighbors and then our city or municipality and our country. To pray in response to the news of the day about a pandemic or crisis that has hit another country. To pray for the local elementary school teachers and the local businesses. For one and all, we are

MANUAL WORK IS SO FREQUENTLY AN IDEAL TIME FOR TENDING TO OUR PRAYERS.

praying that they would flourish in life and work. And we pray for the church where we worship and its various ministries. Those whose work is with their hands are often also the intercessors within the community.

This was perhaps most exemplified in the one who lived this—surely the one who, if there were one, would be the patron saint of those who work with their hands: Brother Lawrence who lived and worked in France in the seventeenth century. Nicolas Herman was born in 1610 and in his adult years served in the French army during the Thirty Years War. In time, he decided to join the local monastery, but he lacked the theological education to become a priest, so he was appointed as a lay brother. And so, he was "Brother Lawrence" and assigned to work in the kitchen: cooking meals and washing dishes. He did this for fifteen years before he was reassigned to repair sandals and shoes. Over time, he was known for his personal integrity, the quality of his work, and his disposition. Many came to visit with him and learn from him, and the collection of his sayings and teachings was published after his death as *The Practice of the Presence of God*, which captured the essential wisdom of his life and work—notably his insistence that he could be and was fully present to God even with his hands in the kitchen sink. His sayings include this line:

> The time of work does not with me differ from the time of worship; and in the noise and clatter of my kitchen, even while several people are at the same time calling out for different things, I commune with God in as great a tranquility as if I were upon my knees in prayer in the holiest cathedral of worship.[5]

What is noteworthy is that the dominant theme of the sayings of Brother Lawrence is the love of God. Again and again, he stresses that in the comings and goings of our daily chores and our work, it is both possible and essential that we live continually aware of the love of God that

WE PRAY NOT AS THOSE IN CONTINUOUS COMPLAINT, BUT WITH A GRATEFUL HEART.

infuses us with a deep and resilient joy. And this is surely the backdrop, then, to our intercessory prayers: we pray not as those in continuous complaint, but with a grateful heart. The spirituality of Brother Lawrence is very much seeking and knowing God in the everyday—not merely in our time of retreat or worship or morning prayer but in the actual rhythms and routines of our work. And typically, those whose primary work is with their hands find they can be fully attentive to their work but also be conscious of the presence of God and able to pray for those whom they love and care for. We need the plumber and the farmer not merely for what they produce; we also depend on their prayers.

QUESTIONS FOR REFLECTION AND DISCUSSION

1. Consider one of the trades—done by yourself or someone you know who works with their hands—and talk about why this work is significant and worthwhile and done with grace, intelligence, and beauty.

2. Describe a project you did—with your hands—and why it was meaningful to you.

3. Is there a tool in your workshop or garden shed that is a source of delight to you—perhaps your favorite tool?

7

VOCATIONAL THINKING
MEANS ORGANIZATIONAL
THINKING

FOR ALL OF US—LITERALLY, for all of us—we only ultimately fulfill our vocations if and as we learn to work with
and within institutions. I need to quickly add that this is not
an overstatement in that some might immediately protest
and try to come up with examples where this is not the case.
If there is an exception, I really doubt it; to the contrary, a
case can be made that for all of us, regardless of our vocation
or calling, we flourish within our calling or vocation if and as
we learn to be organization people: that is, individuals who
know how to work within social structures—institutions—
where our contribution is leveraged against the contributions of others. The writer works with an editor; the farmer
needs a market; the lawyer with a firm; the doctor with a
well-run clinic; the artist with the gallery owner; the professor with colleagues but also with the administrative leadership that work with one and all toward the flourishing of

this institution in this time and this place. No one is a solitary player.

Further, organizations give us an opportunity to contribute to something greater and larger than ourselves—to be part of a movement, to contribute our energies and vision alongside that of others. Our joint impact—working together with a common objective—is exponentially greater than anything any one of us can do alone. We often encounter those who are visionary, passionate about causes that matter to them, and thus eager to make a difference in the world. But what we also often learn is that they, for some reason, view institutions as a drag or obstacle to their vision and ideals for the church or society.[1] They assume the very last thing they need is an institution to get in their way. But could it be that without an organization, nothing really gets done? Might it be that we might have a vision, with a great idea and lots of energy to foster change, but nothing of lasting benefit actually happens?

> OUR JOINT IMPACT—WORKING TOGETHER WITH A COMMON OBJECTIVE—IS EXPONENTIALLY GREATER THAN ANYTHING ANY ONE OF US CAN DO ALONE.

A classic example is the Occupy movement that started with Occupy Wall Street with an agenda to get "money out of politics." Eventually, it spread to eighty-two countries and ended up being a protest moment, inspired by the Arab Spring, that addressed everything from social ills to demands for democracy in Hong Kong. But as cofounder Micah White himself acknowledges in an interview with Susan Cole, it did not achieve its objectives even though it lasted so long and was covered by the news media on the front pages of major periodicals.[2] In Hong Kong, Occupy Central lasted ten months. But in the end, there was nothing to show for all the time and effort. As White observes, this and other Occupy movements may have, to some degree, affected some people on some level, but in the end accomplished little, if anything, of lasting or substantive change. Or as Susan Cole puts in that same interview, to accomplish anything, you have to have some level of organization. Or stating it bluntly, you need to create an institution. It is naive to think otherwise.

For any of us who care about the society or church, who want to make a difference, and who want to see core values informing real life circumstances, we need to learn and know how institutions work and how we can work most effectively within them. If we are going to flourish, vocationally, in our careers—whether paid or as volunteers, whether our work is in the for-profit marketplace or in education, the arts or the church—we need to develop institutional competence: the capacity to work in and be part of leveraging the potential of an organization. We need to develop institutional intelligence: a way of thinking that is as vital and essential as emotional intelligence or any kind of intelligence. We can either fight institutions and view institutions as inherently a problem—out of some sentimental or idealistic notion of what makes for human flourishing—or we can learn how to live with them and work within them. We can develop institutional savvy, understanding how institutions work while learning how we can function most effectively within the organization so that we contribute to its effectiveness.

Thus, we need to ask, If vocational thinking requires organizational thinking, what does it mean to understand and work with this assumption? What does it mean to thrive vocationally within an institution?

FINDING CONGRUENCE

First, when we think about what it means to work within an institution, our greatest capacity or potential for vocational flourishing is to find ourselves located within an organization or institution where we have a high level of personal congruence. Ideally, where the work we do is invested in and leveraged toward a mission or a set of values that reflect our own values and vision.

Many years ago, I participated in a research project where, with a colleague, we conducted interviews with senior and accomplished scholars and professors. We were seeking to get to the question: What are the variables or factors that shape the potential for a long-term and fruitful career in higher education? What were the practices or disciplines informing their routines, and what other aspects of their lives and their work were such that increased the potential for effectiveness and joy over the long haul?

We had our questions, and no doubt many of those questions were relatively easy and straightforward. The answers and responses confirmed what we might have suspected— disciplines, and routines, and approaches to life and work led to their success. But there was one topic that came up that, at first, we thought was secondary—more of an aside. But over the course of the many interviews, we came to see this as a recurring factor: the relationship between the professor and the institution where they taught. And what particularly caught our attention was how they spoke about the high degree of congruency they felt between their own vocation and their personal core values, and those of the institution where they were serving. This relationship, while perhaps not perfect, was nevertheless generative. One senior professor stressed he had struggled to fit in at two schools before he ended up at Regent College in Vancouver, British Columbia. There was nothing wrong with the other schools; it was merely that it took him a while to find a place or venue where he could flourish. And he stressed that he was glad he didn't take on an attitude where he would insist on making it work and would work on his scholarship and keep his head low and do all he could to make the best of it. Rather, he concluded he needed to take the risk and make the move to find himself where there was a high level of congruence between himself and the mission and values of the organization, where he then lived out his work as a scholar and teacher.

In an acknowledgments section of one of his publications, James K. A. Smith speaks of his gratitude to the school where he teaches, Calvin College, and he notes that he is "nested" there.[3] The image of being nested might perhaps be misconstrued by some, except there is no perfect metaphor and we need ways of speaking about our relationship with organizations that goes beyond either membership— perhaps in a club or church—or employment, where the relationship is contractual. Both membership and em- ployment are legitimate: to be a member of this political party, to be employed by this firm. Both are good and legitimate. But when we speak of institutions and vocation, we are thinking in terms of how our identity, values, and vision for life and work are found within an organization that allows us to work with others toward a common goal or objective and where we know two things.

First, that we will only fulfill our own vocations when we have a generative relationship with this organization—the organization animates us, refines us, and calls forth our best. Yes, for sure, institutions and denominations can be quite discouraging, and we want to throw up our hands and give up and walk away in frustration. No relationship with an organization or a denomination will be perfect; and thus, we come to some acceptance, some resolution, and work to thrive—and even flourish—as part of something bigger than ourselves. Which leads naturally to this next point.

Second, an organization gives us an opportunity to do our part, but to do so alongside others with complementary talents and abilities, so that with mutually supportive and interdependent skills and contributions we make a difference far greater than we could accomplish on our own. We need the talents of others: the writer with the editor, the university professor who knows she needs this organization to have a capable CFO because she does not have that range of skills or competencies. We come to see that we each do our part, we each contribute, but we do so as part of a greater whole.

Now it is important to stress that we will never find one-to-one congruence between our personal vision and that of the organization where we serve and of which we are a part. We will not find the perfect denomination for our church membership; we will not secure a job or get an assignment with an organization that has everything lined up precisely like we would like it to be. The exception, if there is one, would be for those who actually founded the denomination or organization or company. *Perhaps.* I say "perhaps" in that the very best of those who start something new—a new company or business, a new denomination—very early on lean into the wisdom and expertise of others. Martin Luther needed Philip Melanchthon, who was the premier theologian of early Lutheranism, as just one example. But the main point is this. We are not looking for perfection; we are looking for a high enough degree of congruence such that we can be effective—giving of our time and energy, knowing that with the investment of our talent and resolve, we are contributing to something bigger than ourselves.

This is not always possible. Sometimes we just need a job; we need to get a regular paycheck. Or perhaps we know we need to be somewhere on Sunday morning even if the only option for worship in our neighborhood or town is with a church that is of a rather different ilk than what we might otherwise choose. And we graciously accept this limitation. But, to the degree that it is possible, we need to pursue congruence and ideally do so sooner than later. The best would be that as we move into our forties, we have done enough experimentation and we have come to a high enough level of self-knowledge to know where we belong. And if we can find it, it has the potential to make all the difference in the world to our vocational journey.

WORKING EFFECTIVELY WITH OTHERS

We need to speak to the importance of congruence. But then, further, we have to appreciate that the only way we will thrive within an institution is if and as we develop the capacity to work effectively with others. Organizations by their very nature are social entities where cooperation, collaboration, and coordination are essential capacities.

The ability to work with others is, without doubt, one of the most essential elements to thriving in an organization, which means, then, that it is essential to vocational flourishing. We will not be effective in fulfilling our calling unless and until we learn to work with others. We learn as children what it means to play with others—refusing to bully or be bullied, learning to share, joining in games as a peer and contributor. In school, we hopefully learn that this is not about competition but that we can find deep joy in joint projects and assignments where our understanding and ability are complemented by that of another. Team sports are also an opportunity to learn what it means to be dependent on others and to be dependable, to contribute our skill but to do so as a way to coordinate with others such that together we accomplish something we cannot or could not accomplish alone.

The point is that sooner than later, this is part of who we are: we know how to lead and how to follow; we know how to listen; we know how to do what it behooves us to do if the group or team or organization is going to succeed. We know how to find particular joy when an outcome—a win or a completed project—is clearly one that could only happen because we worked together toward a common outcome.

There are no heroes. We each do our part. We each contribute. We leverage our diverse strengths—and compensate for our limitations—by leaning into the strengths of others.

If you are a writer, the strength and capacity of your writing will be exponentially greater if you learn how to work with an editor. If you are a pastor, you learn how to work with a board chair and with the person who is the church treasurer and with your colleagues on the pastoral leadership team. You also learn what it means to work with volunteers. If you are in politics,

> WE LEVERAGE OUR DIVERSE STRENGTHS—AND COMPENSATE FOR OUR LIMITATIONS—BY LEANING INTO THE STRENGTHS OF OTHERS.

you cultivate the capacity to develop legislation that has a significant measure of bipartisan support—legislation you are actually developing together across the political aisle. This means you know something of the give and take—of listening and learning together and deferring to one another and knowing it is not always about getting your own way but working, with energy and commitment, toward a *shared* vision of what we are seeking to accomplish. Organizations only work—and we only thrive within them—if we learn to work together with others.

ORGANIZATIONAL ATTENTIVENESS

We can speak specifically to what it means to be attentive to the particular organization in which we find ourselves—be that a church, a school, a political party, a business, or a nonprofit agency. We need to consider at the very least five things: the mission, the historical location, the system of governance, the ethos or culture, and then also we need to ask the accountability question. If we thrive as part of organizations, it is as if we develop an attentiveness to these dimensions and learn to operate accordingly.

First, we ask: What is the mission of this organization, and how can I contribute effectively to this mission? Our involvement and our personal vocation might well be bigger than the mission, however it is defined. That is, our identity is not co-opted by or limited by the mission. But, at the very least, we know the mission, we work with others to achieve that mission, and we respectfully do not work in ways that are at counter purposes to that mission.

I need to, however, add an important caveat: Do not assume the mission is either limited by a mission statement or limited by the particular articulation of the mission by whoever happens to be in senior leadership at this time. Yes, it is imperative that those in senior leadership roles recognize that part of their responsibility is to highlight the mission, celebrate that mission, and with accountability to the board keep the organization on mission. But leaders should not presume they are the only ones who know or articulate the mission. We can be a member of a local church and really feel the current leadership is not understanding or articulating the mission effectively. A professor might be frustrated that the president seems to have an overly narrow conception of what it means to be this university. In other words, there is a place for an honest disagreement or a diversity of perspective. But, to function effectively, on some level at least we need to be on board and able to work with others toward a common objective. We live and work well when we are aware of the organizational purpose of this entity, this institution.

Second, when we think about organizations, we need to stress that all organizations are located in a particular time and place. Michael Jinkins and Deborah Bradshaw Jinkins state it well when speaking of leadership, but this principle applies to all of us, regardless of our specific roles or responsibilities within the organization. They write:

> Leadership is always grounded in a particular time and place—in a particular culture. And the effective leader inevitably maintains a connection with *this* specific time and place, *this* culture, leading *these* people in *this* moment—a connection that is as elusive as it is real.[4]

As noted, this applies to all of us: We are part of organizations located in this time and in this place. We work within institutions with colleagues, and we have shared circumstances, shared limitations, and shared opportunities. And no amount of wishing it otherwise is going to change this. This is now our location—this time, this place. And what we all need from one another is an attentiveness to both the limits and the opportunities this brings—regardless of your particular role within the organization.

Third, when we are attentive to an organization and our location or role within it, this necessarily means that we have a basic understanding of the system or approach to governance of this organization. If we want to make a difference and be vocationally effective through an organization and in partnership with others in an organization, we cannot afford to be naive on this score or assume that matters of politics, governance, and decision-making are beneath us or not relevant to us.

If you are called into any level of civic responsibility, you will only make a constructive difference if you know how that system of governance works—in your city or country. In the United States, if you are called into politics, you know the history of and the content of the Constitution and how Congress works and how legislation is passed. In the United Kingdom or Canada, you have a parliamentary system of governance, and you function accordingly. In a church, a congregational system of governance is rather different from an episcopal approach to decision-making. You work with and within the system; you know how decisions are made in this organization and you know how to contribute to the decision-making process. In a university or a non-profit or a college, you have your calling, but you are invested in contributing to the shared vision for *this* place and *this* organization, and so you learn and work within the system of governance. You know how it works; you know your part in the process. You know the protocols. And if you are on a committee, you know how that committee works. That is, you know how to work on a committee—how to make an active and helpful contribution with attention to the protocols of good committee work. But you also know the specifics of this committee's responsibility: Does it have executive authority to make decisions, or does it only submit recommendations to another entity?

Knowing how to function on a committee within an organization is a basic vocational competency. This is not a distraction or a rude interference into your life and work and vocation; rather, if you recognize your calling and work are located within an organization, you will know how to work within the system of governance and decision-making of this particular agency. And that almost always means knowing how to function effectively within a moderated deliberative process—in a committee.

And fourth, those who are organizationally attentive also understand the power and significance of institutional culture. Vibrant and effective organizations have a culture that is dynamic—marked by hope, creativity, joy, and resilience. It is no doubt the case that senior leadership play a key role in this regard: to speak hope within complex and difficult circumstances, sustaining a vision for innovation as they foster the capacity of the organization to adapt and respond to new developments. But it is important to stress that all those who are part of an organization have a part to play in the way they are present to and encourage their colleagues and those whom they serve. We can all ask, as part of our vocational identity and calling: What can I do today to say thank-you, to encourage a colleague, to work with others to sustain a vision for life and work that makes this a good place to be investing our time and energy?

And fifth, those who are organizationally attentive are able to answer the accountability question. We each need to be accountable for the quality and character of our work. And this means we should have clarity on the question: To whom am I accountable? A poet or artist or scholar to their guild. Two artists who paint together and call forth the best in each other. A faculty member of a university who submits her course syllabus for approval and teaches and does her research on the assumption that she is accountable to her disciplinary guild and to the dean and her faculty colleagues for the quality and character of her work. A pastor and senior leader of a nonprofit reports to a board and is intentionally accountable to the board for the quality of the work for which this person is responsible. This is actually a gift, not a burdensome problem or imposition. We will only thrive within and through our callings—our vocations—when we work and live with intentional accountability for our work. This does not mean we are not self-directed; it does not mean we are only effective when someone is looking over our shoulder. Accountability does not mean there is someone nagging us or continually on our case. Rather, the genius of accountability is someone who affirms us and our work but will not flatter us and will work with us to nudge us and call us to do our best work in light of the very standards we have set for ourselves.

WE EMBRACE AND ARE FULLY PRESENT— AND WE LEARN TO LET GO

When we speak about organizations, one of the key indicators of vocational maturity and effectiveness is that we are fully present to the organization—engaged and committed—but then also, we are able to let go and leave when that time comes. On the one hand we are invested: we are present, to this place, to this group of colleagues, to this mission. We participate with generosity of heart toward our shared organizational purpose. But then, it also means this: we know when it is time to step aside, resign, retire. Think of it this way: our life and work within organizations is as a series of hellos and goodbyes. Organizations mean new assignments, new opportunities, new responsibilities, new challenges; each time, each new beginning, is a time to say hello and engage a new situation with eagerness. But then, we also know that living and working in organizations includes learning to say goodbye. Just as at home, children grow up and move into adulthood; just as deaths intersect our lives—sometimes expected and other times more tragically. Even so, colleagues retire, we retire, we sell the business, we move on. We say hello, but just as surely, we also learn to say goodbye.

Sometimes, this is not our decision. We are asked to resign, or we are let go. That can be a very difficult moment in our career. And it will happen to many, if not most of us, at some point. At other times, of course, there is such a thing as limited tenure. The president of the United States can only serve two four-year terms. It is assumed there is then a transition as one graciously leaves office to other pursuits. Perhaps you are serving on a board—a church or nonprofit board— that has limited tenure. And, frankly, all healthy and effective boards have a policy that assumes limited tenure: that is, there is a season to be fully present and there is a time when we step aside and let others pick up the baton. In these cases, vocational integrity requires that we accept this transition and step aside: graciously, willingly, and with affirmation and blessing for our successors.

But then also, we can speak of those situations when it is more in our control to identify the time when we would step aside and embrace a new role or opportunity. Sometimes this can be quite a difficult challenge; we have decided that our current work situation, for whatever reason, is no longer tenable. At other times, we have enjoyed this work and been effective in this organization, but it is time—and we know it is time, even though there may be sadness—to accept that it is time to leave. Part of effective vocational discernment is realizing we may need to take the initiative and resign. This should not be easy; we do not want to merely quit because the situation is difficult or challenging. We need to affirm the value of perseverance and persistence. And yet the time will come when we discern the time has come. Perhaps we have completed what we believe we came to this job to accomplish. Or, alternatively, we have reached an impasse and because of some significant limitation—perhaps the political dynamics of our job—we make the move. We do not romanticize the alternative; and yet, we make the move because it is the right thing to do as an act of courage and commitment and humility.

Sometimes we leave because we recognize the hard reality that staying achieves nothing. We have come up against the proverbial brick wall and realize that little is gained and much is lost by staying on out of a false sense of duty when in our heart we know "there is no future here."

But also, in this, we are resolved to not overstay. We have made our contribution and now, whether in a paid position or on a church board or in a volunteer agency, whether or not there is a limited tenure policy, we graciously relinquish the role and responsibility. When we have been with the organization an appropriate length of time, we move on; we retire, resign, let go. We resolve to not overstay. We do not cling to a job or appointment beyond our effective date or, as one person put it to me, beyond our "shelf life."

And I will add one more point that is relevant regardless of the terms of our departure—happy or sad. As the older expression puts it: do not burn your bridges; you will not know if you will need a bridge to return to the other side at some point in the future. Even if the departure is particularly difficult or onerous, leave as graciously as possible. Nothing, absolutely nothing, is gained by trying to score points on the way out the door. When you leave on the best possible terms, surprises so frequently come your way— perhaps years later as you are asked to make a contribution or even, in some cases, to come back into the employ of that same organization. Don't burn bridges on the way out the door. Leave a blessing.

THE CRITICAL NEED FOR DIFFERENTIATION

If we are effective within an organization, it comes as we embrace the mission and invest our hearts and minds in the shared values and vision of the institution. But it is also important that we sustain some level of personal autonomy. We are not reduced to our roles within the organization. Our identity and our calling are never solely that of one who fills a role within this church or business or school. We *are* invested; we do give ourselves generously and even sacrificially to and for and with our colleagues toward a shared and common vision for what it is that we are trying to accomplish. And yet our identity is not so tied up with the organization that we feel we need to be in on every decision or that we cannot serve eagerly after we got outvoted at a committee meeting. We give of ourselves but always sustain a gracious otherness: not that we are aloof but rather that our joys and sorrows are not linked one-to-one to the organization. And this means that when the time comes, we can graciously let go and move on—to another assignment or into our senior years—able to freely trust and entrust the organization to others who will carry the collective vision and values going forward.

We can only do this, of course, if we take personal responsibility for our lives and are not overly beholden to the organization or equate our lives with the organization. This is only possible if we are able to know the grace and disposition of what developmental theorists speak of as *differentiation*.

To this end, we need to speak to one of the most crucial and sensitive of all issues when it comes to the interconnection of our vocation—our personal calling—and the institution in which and with which we invest time and energy. There are two dangers or inclinations that need to be avoided. The first is that the institution or the organization is merely a platform or paycheck for us to be able to do what we want to do. Our relation to the organization is, one might say, somewhat parasitic: we take and give back the minimum, no more than is necessary. We are not truly invested or committed to the shared agenda, the common sense of purpose; we are merely along for the ride.

The other danger or inclination is to make a one-to-one correlation between ourselves and our personal vocation and the mission of the organization. We are a company person; we have no other life or awareness of our life purpose than this organization in which we have invested our lives and for which we are willing and eager to be not only present, but 100 percent invested. There is a sense in which we have actually subsumed our identity and vocation within the mission of this organization. We cannot imagine our lives except as part of this church, this company, or this nonprofit organization. And the danger with this inclination is twofold.

First, institutions are notoriously tough places—financially and politically. You may be on the good side of the boss or the employer today, but when the finances are tight or the politics are messy, the fact that you have been loyal and effective and diligent is all good, but it may not, in the end, keep you from having to face the reality that your position is being terminated. When it comes to vocation and our sense of personal identity and purpose, it is essential that we not only realize institutions are the necessary venue for hosting or housing our vocation, but also realize that institutions are contingent. The practical and political dynamics of all organizations mean we need to be present but also hold lightly and learn how to live graciously with the inevitable: we will transition out by our own choice or we will be transitioned.

In other words, the genius of institutional engagement is found, at least in part, in living with this tension—this dynamic. We are fully present, fully engaged. But we are not married to the organization or institution. Our identity and sense of purpose is not dependent on whether or not we have this particular job with this particular organization. And for this, it

> WE ARE FULLY PRESENT, FULLY ENGAGED. BUT WE ARE NOT MARRIED TO THE ORGANIZATION OR INSTITUTION.

is imperative that all along the way we do not equate our vocations with this institution and, further, that our ego needs are not tied to the specific job or role we have within the organization. We can let it go. The bottom line remains: we take ownership of our own lives and thus take responsibility to steward our own sense of identity and purpose, even as we serve within an organization with generosity, diligence, and humility.

QUESTIONS FOR REFLECTION AND DISCUSSION

1. Within your current position and place of work, what are the key stress points you need to manage with wisdom, patience, and grace? And how are these fostering within you a greater capacity for faith, hope, and love?

2. What—for you—is a particular source of joy in the organization where you are currently employed, or where, as a volunteer, are you investing your time and energy?

8

PRACTICES
OF ENGAGEMENT

IN THE HISTORY OF CHRISTIAN SPIRITUALITY, it has been
common to make a distinction between the *contemplative*
life or vocation and its counterpart, the *active* life—that is,
the calling or vocation to be in the world. For much of that
history, the contemplative life—the vocation or calling to
prayer and study—was viewed to be a higher or more superior calling. But Christian spirituality at its best affirms
both. The focus of this book is the active life: the work to
which we are called, in this time and in this place. It is
helpful to speak of the active life as an essential counterpart to the contemplative life. But more, it is typically
assumed that the contemplative life means those practices
that draw us into fellowship with God. And yet, what
perhaps needs highlighting is how the active life is equally
a means by which we grow in faith and mature in our
Christian identity. But this is only so when we are intentional. And to this end, I will invite you to consider *practices*

of engagement—spiritual practices that complement the practices of the contemplative life.

THE INSTRUCTIVE HISTORY OF RELIGIOUS ORDERS

When we consider the meaning of vocation against the backdrop of the merits of the contemplative life versus the active life, it is helpful to do a very brief history of religious orders. For the ancient sixth century Benedictine monastic tradition, there is no doubt they were in retreat from the world—isolated in a community governed by prayer. Even with their affirmation of both study and manual work, prayer was their ultimate calling. Indeed, some monastic orders emerging from the ancient Benedictine vision very intentionally foster seclusion and isolation: communities of prayer that are obviously not "in the world."

But something significant shifted with the establishing of the aptly called mendicant orders early in the thirteenth century: inspired by their respective founders, Dominicans and Franciscans, while still monastic in their common and shared life, were very much "in the city." It is typical that Dominican and Franciscan houses of prayer and worship are located within the very heart of the city. As a young person growing up in Ecuador, I came to appreciate that these two orders, along with the Augustinians, were located right in the heart of old Quito, the capital. What guided their vocations was an ancient line, which was actually the motto of the Dominicans: *contemplata aliis tradit*—to hand on to others, to share, the fruit of contemplation. It is a perspective that comes from the leading Dominican theologian, Saint Thomas Aquinas, who, writing later in the thirteenth century, insisted the contemplative life is superior to the active life, but that it behooves those called into the so-called contemplative life to be in generous service for God, in the world, in the heart of the city, sharing the benefits of the grace they have come to know through the rhythms and practices of the contemplative life.[1]

So much of this perspective was based on a particular reading of the contrast made between Mary and Martha (Lk 10), and how in their encounter with Jesus, Mary is affirmed as having "chosen the better way"—sitting at the feet of Jesus as attentive disciple—while Martha seems to have missed the better way as she is active in the kitchen. This is not an accurate read of this text; Martha was not called out of the kitchen. Her problem or limitation was not that she was engaged in what we might speak of as the active life. But this was often used as a basis for assuming the contemplative life was the superior way, and that the only meaning to the active life was as a means of sharing the fruits of contemplation.

> WE ARE CALLED TO BOTH—THE CONTEMPLATIVE LIFE AND THE ACTIVE LIFE, THE LIFE OF PRAYER AND COMMUNION WITH GOD AS WELL AS GENEROUS SERVICE FOR GOD IN THE WORLD.

We are called to both—the contemplative life and the active life, the life of prayer and communion with God as well as generous service for God in the world. Though the focus of this book is the active life, we can learn from these traditions of Christian spirituality and affirm that we lose a sense of calling and vocation when we are overengaged, without boundaries or clarity about our calling or a clear sense of our vocational priorities. We need the time and space of sabbath disengagement, personal prayer, corporate worship, and other related spiritual practices that anchor and sustain our distinctive identity as children of God—as such that we are regularly away, in retreat and in solitude, as the essential precondition and counterpart to our lives of generous service in the world.

And yet, we need to go further and not only affirm the active life, but also speak to how it is a means by which we are drawn into fellowship with God. For this we can turn to the sixteenth century and the remarkable vision of Saint Ignatius Loyola, founder of the Society of Jesus—the Jesuits. Ignatius was convinced that Christians are called to be in the world in generous service—thus affirming a vocation or calling to the active life. He did not discount the importance of prayer, contemplation, and retreat. Not for a moment. But he did not assume that we know and find God in retreat and in prayer, and then "merely" share the fruit or benefit of this contemplation in the world. Rather—and this is the radical piece, simply revolutionary—he went further and insisted that while we find God in prayer, we also meet God and know the grace of God in the world. That is, in the language of the early Jesuits, we go into the world "finding God in all things." God goes before us, God meets us, God's grace is present to us, yes, in prayer, but *also* in the world—in the work, the relationships, the encounters, and the social and cultural circumstances in which we are called. We find God in the neighborhood, in the office, in the marketplace. We find God in both prayer and in our places and spaces of work in the world.

Many years later, Dietrich Bonhoeffer in his *Life Together* would observe that both give meaning and integrity to the other: we go into the world as pray-ers (those who pray) and we go into our prayers

> **PRAYER IS NOT SUPERIOR TO WORK, BUT IT IS THE ESSENTIAL COUNTERPART TO OUR WORK, JUST AS WORK IS THE ESSENTIAL COUNTERPART TO OUR PRAYERS.**

as those who have been in the world. Prayer is not superior to work, but it is the essential counterpart to our work, just as work is the essential counterpart to our prayers. Or, as Bonhoeffer puts it:

> Praying and working are two different things. Prayer should not be hindered by work, but neither should work be hindered by prayer. . . . Every day should be marked for the Christian both by prayer and work. . . . Without the burden and labor of the day, prayer is not prayer; and without prayer, work is not work.[2]

Prayer is not the only way that we meet God or know God or are in fellowship with God. Prayer is essential; it is a vital means by which we know the grace of God and, as such, necessary to our work—essential to what it is we are called to do and to our knowledge of God. But the point is that it is not the *only* means by which we know God and know the grace of God. We also meet God "in the world."

FINDING GRACE IN THE WORLD

We often speak of spiritual practices that foster the life of prayer, contemplation, and communion with God—in worship, in retreat, in sabbath rest, and in disengagement from the world so that we know the grace of God that sustains us for the life, work, and witness to which we are called. But if grace is not only found in retreat and in prayer through practices of disengagement, what are the counterpart practices of engagement by which we know the grace of God in the world? To stress: we are not merely seeking grace to be in the world; rather, we are actually knowing the grace of God in the world, very specifically through what we see and experience in the world. But for this, as with contemplation, we need to be intentional. Thus, we speak of practices by which we know the grace of God in the world.

It is helpful to speak of four—there are more, of course, but at the very least four—practices of engagement: hospitality, acts of mercy, financial giving, and intercessory prayer. Each of these has value in its own right, needing no justification. But the focus here is how each of these is a practice by which our identity and work and engagement in the world comes to greater clarity and, in particularly, greater alignment with the purposes of God in the world.

That is, when we speak of "spiritual practice" we speak of a means to an end: to know the grace of God in Christ. But we can be more specific and ask, What grace? That is, what grace do we seek through this or the other spiritual practice? Rather than merely assuming we want to grow in faith, hope, and love—which is, of course, a very good thing—more to the point we ask: What dimension or aspect of faith, hope, and love is being cultivated in us through a particular spiritual practice? How can we cultivate what we might speak of as vocational holiness?

First and fundamentally, we can speak of hearts and minds and lives that are aligned with Christ and his kingdom. This is always the bottom line: that as God enables, our words and our deeds are means by which we live and work, speak and act, in a way that is congruent with the benevolent reign of Christ in our lives and in our world.

Second, and the natural counterpart to this, is that we would become less concerned with our own identity and success, that we would live in the freedom that comes with living a decentered life, where our life and work are ultimately about Christ and about others and not about ourselves. Yes, of course, vocation is about the stewardship of our lives; but in the end, it is not about us. We need practices that cultivate within us the courage to do the right thing, but also the grace and patience to not be obsessed with our reputation or how others appreciate us. And this includes accepting that some of the most significant work we do is done in obscurity.

And then, third, all work and witness in our world comes ideally from an attentiveness to where Christ is acting and where the Spirit is present. That is, we need practices that open our eyes and ears to the cries of the children, the pain of a fragmented world, and with this, the possibilities that might emerge to witness the grace of God in a particular context and setting.

To this end, seeking this grace—vocational holiness—consider the place of these four spiritual practices of *engagement*: engagement with the world, through our work and alongside the work to which we are called. It is helpful to think of there being four distinct practices that foster our capacity—regardless of our specific calling or vocation—to live and work with an attentiveness to the presence of Christ in the world and, further, to decenter ourselves and cut the nerve of narcissism and self-obsession.

HOSPITALITY

Following up on the comments about the trajectory of religious orders, here we can and should highlight the Benedictine contribution to this spiritual practice. The ancient Rule of Saint Benedict affirmed the rhythm of manual labor, study, and prayer; and yet, there was also an assumption that when it came to the outside world, that point of contact between the monastic community and the world was marked by a commitment to hospitality. The link to the world was mediated, one might say, through the practice of radical hospitality. Chapter 53 of the Rule affirmed: "All guests who present themselves are to be welcomed as Christ, for himself will say, 'I was a stranger and you welcomed me' (Mt 25:35). Proper honor must be shown to all, 'especially those who share our faith' (Gal 6:10) and to pilgrims."[3]

Could it be that in a similar vein, hospitality both precedes all points of engagement with the world—anticipates and sets the stage for what we say and what we do—and, further, is necessarily intertwined with all our ways of fulfilling our respective vocations? That is, for everyone—regardless of their vocation—hospitality is an essential spiritual practice. It is a way of being. And, further, it is in each time and each place, a disposition: the rhythms and routines that foster a distinctive openness to the other— meeting the other as and where they are—and in meeting the other, being open to the possibility of fellowship with the other.

There is a place for the welcome associated with the church that is eager for new worshippers, or a university that welcomes prospective students for a tour of the campus, or a restaurant or business that establishes a tenor of welcome to a client or customer. But the heart of the matter is captured so well by Henri Nouwen when he speaks of hospitality as *creating space*. It is not about changing another person but creating space where change might happen, including new learning.[4] But what Nouwen insists is that in essence what is happening is that we move from being strangers, in fear of hostility, to becoming friends—or at least opening up the possibility of friendship.

The Scriptures seem to assume a kind of concentric circle approach to the practice of hospitality. We begin with the church community; we are hospitable to one another (1 Pet 4:9), recognizing this commitment and the priority that is justifiably given to our hospitality to each other within the church (Gal 6:10). How can we be hospitable to others if we do not welcome one another? We begin here. But this hospitality is never exclusive; it is not about us and is not true hospitality until and unless it is expressed toward the outsider, the stranger, the "other." Even within the church, hospitality by definition means we respond with generosity to those who are different—whether it was for the apostolic church, with the generous response of Jews toward Gentiles and Gentiles toward Jews, or for us today, it surely means a hospitality across social, ethnic, racial differences. And more, it means specifically we are hospitable toward those with whom we differ, potentially on substantive matters—as we see in the call of Paul to the church in Rome, in Romans 14 and then the grand conclusion to that call in Romans 15:7. Our hospitality is always a reflection of the hospitality of God toward us; we, as Paul puts it, welcome one another as Christ has welcomed us. Thus, hospitality is a living expression or embodiment of the gospel. If we truly believe and feel God has shown us a generous hospitality, it will be evident in our hospitality toward another.

But we need to go one step further. It is often assumed that if we are hospitable, it is out of generosity—which it is—but more, that it is charitable: out of our position of security (and perhaps even wealth and comfort), we are hospitable toward the traveler, the refugee, the immigrant, the person whose views or whose actions are somehow viewed as lesser and therefore require hospitality.

EVEN WITHIN THE CHURCH, HOSPITALITY BY DEFINITION MEANS WE RESPOND WITH GENEROSITY TO THOSE WHO ARE DIFFERENT.

That as God was hospitable to us, now we—from a position of being "insiders" (like God and with God)—offer hospitality toward the other. There is an element of truth here. However, it is vital that we appreciate true hospitality, realizing that in and through acts of hospitality we put ourselves in a posture or disposition or place where we have the potential to not only give, but also receive. We are hospitable to the other not only that they might have their needs met—for safety, for food, or compassion, or love—but so we also learn and grow as our horizons are broadened: we come to a greater knowledge and understanding of truth. We are enriched; we see or witness or experience another dimension of the goodness and grace of God and of God's truth.

And so, Nouwen insists hospitality always means the possibility we will learn and we will be changed. He uses strong language here: "Reaching out to others without being receptive to them is more harmful than helpful and easily leads to manipulation and even to violence, violence in thoughts, words and actions."[5] The main point here is we do not offer hospitality if and only if the other agrees with us or believes as we believe.

The Scriptures speak of how Abraham and Sarah welcomed three strangers and in so doing welcomed angels (or did they welcome the triune God? [Gen 18]). This question is revisited in the book of Hebrews where we are urged to show hospitality to strangers, for in so doing, we might welcome an angel without knowing it (Heb 13:2). Might it be that every act of hospitality is for us a means by which, in our engagement with the world, through the other— whether neighbor or stranger, whether immigrant or political or theological adversary (someone with whom we differ on a substantive matter)—in some mysterious way we see God afresh and the ways of God in the world through new eyes? And, in so doing, have greater insight into all of life and, in particular, our vocations?

The church welcomes the immigrant and the refugee and discovers a new cuisine, no doubt, but more to the point, they come to see God and the ways of God from a different angle. The university professor's hospitality toward a student opens up a way of reading a text or seeing a problem in a manner she had not seen before. Every year, then, every teaching of this course, always has the question, offered in hospitality to this cohort of students: What new insight into the topic or theme of this course might arise? That is, we encounter Christ in the guise of the other—the stranger, the neighbor, even the adversary. Are there boundaries? Without doubt. But they are flexible limits and give space for the other to learn and grow and change.

And so, we might consider again the remarkable words of Paul in Romans 14 and 15. The Roman church was deeply divided on two substantive matters—likely though not necessarily divided along ethnic lines. They differed and likely viewed the oppositional view as questioning their own faith and the integrity of their own spiritual experience.[6] What amazes us is that the apostle Paul did not in his response to them resolve the difference—the theological, moral, and spiritual questions they were wrestling with. Why? First, I suspect because he knew differences would always mark the life of the church and they needed to learn how to differ and do so graciously. They needed to learn how to manage being the church when there were ongoing differences of opinion. They needed to learn to "welcome one another . . . just as Christ has welcomed you" (Rom 15:7) even if they had not resolved their differences. That is, they welcome one another in the meantime recognizing they might never actually agree.

They need to get beyond any idea that we only offer a welcome to another if and when they agree with us.

But more, I wonder this—if there is another reason why he did not resolve this for them: that we always need to be open and attentive and willing to engage others, so there is always the possibility of new learning, new vistas. Perhaps we need to always be attentive to those with whom we differ because it keeps us open and alert to the ways in which we might be called to learn, grow, expand our capacity for compassion. And further, to not become insular—only reading those who agree with us, only listening to those who agree with our perspective, only willing to be in conversation with those who share our convictions.

And so, bottom line: hospitality is an essential spiritual practice of engagement that, as a regular habit and rhythm of our lives, keeps us attentive to the ways in which God is present in the world and expands our vision for how we, in our work, are participants in what God is doing in the world.

WORKS OF MERCY

When the current Pope chose the name "Francis" as his papal designation, following on from his predecessor who had been named Benedict, he made it explicit that he did so out of reverence and respect for the founder of the Franciscan order for whom the poor of the world were his focus and primary concern. As Pope Francis put it, he chose this name because, quite simply, he wanted to remind the church and all Christians we cannot forget the poor. If hospitality is central to the defining identity of the Benedictines, surely the counterpart for the Franciscans is precisely this—the very thing Pope Francis sought in choosing this name: to be for—advocating for and caring for—the poor and the needy in our communities, our cities, and our world—taking to heart the words of Jesus:

> Then the king will say to those at his right hand, "Come, you that are blessed by my Father, inherit the kingdom prepared for you from the foundation of the world; for I was hungry and you gave me food, I was thirsty and you gave me something to drink, I was a stranger and you welcomed me, I was naked and you gave me clothing, I was sick and you took care of me, I was in prison and you visited me." (Mt 25:34-36)

It is deeply unfortunate that as I write these words, the whole notion or idea of caring for the poor and advocating for those who are in need has become politicized. Without doubt, this is a political issue; we need to foster societies and communities marked by a commitment to care for those who struggle to keep food on the table, a roof over their heads, children clothed and cared for. We do need to ask the politically loaded question: Are we attentive to the health and well-being of those in prison? Surely, this vision, this commitment that we cannot forget the poor, is of necessity embraced by all Christians, regardless of their political leanings.

Surely, a congregation that preaches the gospel will, in like fashion, be a community of faith that reflects the gospel in their shared lives and the ways in which, individually and collectively, they are asking: Where are the poor, in need, homeless, and imprisoned in our neighborhoods, and in what practical and tangible ways are we present to them, advocating for them, and responding to their immediate needs? There is the immediacy of the aptly called "Good Samaritan" who responded in the moment: a crisis presented itself and he responded—he had the margin or space in his life that he could respond, on the road, to a fellow in need. Perhaps indeed it could be said that we are never so busy we are not capable of peripheral vision—to see, in the course of our daily lives, the need of another to which we can and must respond. But there is more. This is also a practice, something that is potentially a routine or habit in our lives—not merely the crisis we come upon, but also the ways in which weekly we are finding ways to be present to those in need: serving soup on Thursday nights to the homeless, the regular visit to the prison, the persistent advocacy with city hall for affordable housing for those with limited means.

In all of this, of course, we are Christ to and in our world. But something else is happening. We not only "share the fruits of contemplation," the grace we know through our personal encounter with Christ in prayer and in our spiritual practices of sabbath and Scripture reading, but—and this is the key here—we also meet Christ in the eyes and experience of the poor, as Jesus himself makes clear in the Matthew text previously referenced.

Here it is fruitful to turn to the way in which John Wesley, eighteenth century preacher and writer, not only calls the church toward what he spoke of as "works of mercy" but also to an appreciation that this form of engagement in the world is, to use Wesley's language, a "means of grace." It was John Wesley's conviction that the church and the individual

Christian need to be attentive to the ways by which we can lean into and appropriate the redeeming grace of God. This includes the obvious "means"—notably the ministry of the Word and the Lord's Table—by which the Spirit of God brought the Christian community into greater union with Christ. Wesley recognized that while Word and Table are central—and thus spoke of works of piety, including the sacraments, but also personal prayer, fasting, and the study of the Scriptures—he further referenced works of mercy as also a means of grace: means by which the Spirit is gracing the Christian community.[7]

By this, Wesley means everything from visiting the sick and those in prison, to feeding and clothing the poor. But further, he assumed that in his context this meant opposition to slavery. And surely for the heirs of Wesley, this would include advocating for racial justice, especially when racism has an economic consequence. But mainly this: Wesley speaks of how through works of mercy, the Christian community is not only sharing the grace of God with others, with the needy, but that through these acts we are drawn into the grace and presence of God in the world. These are practices by which we are brought into greater affinity with the presence of Christ and the witness of the Spirit in our world.

Within the Catholic spiritual tradition, there is typically reference made to seven works of mercy: to feed the hungry, give water to the thirsty, clothe the naked, shelter the homeless, care for the sick, visit those in prison, and bury the dead. In Naples, Italy, a church was established that was dedicated to this vision of generosity toward those in need:

the Church of the Pio Monte della Misericordia. Those who had this vision for this church commissioned the painter Caravaggio to provide the major art piece over the altar—a painting he finished circa 1607 portraying all seven of these works of mercy. We see the genius of Caravaggio's use of light infusing the painting, reflecting the conviction that the light of God is shown through works of mercy to and for the needy, but also that those who are instruments of these works of mercy know this grace, the light of God.

We can celebrate the vision of the founders of this church and thus ask—using the more ancient "works of mercy" or the list John Wesley spoke of: How, and in what ways, is God inviting us to participate within our immediate communities and in our world in what God is doing in response to those in need? I think of a dentist who spends two weeks a year providing free dental care for Nicaraguan refugees in Costa Rica. I think of my mother who, a little distressed her own church did not have this ministry, made a weekly trek to another church of a tradition that in her youth "did not preach the gospel" but gave her a chance each week to serve in a soup line. I think of a colleague who while with me at a conference in Thailand, was up early morning each day to visit the local prison, where he knew of Vietnamese pastors who fled Vietnam and were now imprisoned in Thailand because they had entered the country illegally. I think of the seminary in North Park that offers a full regimen of theological courses at the local prison for "lifers." And of the congregation in Surrey, British Columbia, who dedicate a whole wing of their facility to providing shelter and breakfast on "the coldest night of the year."

Can we ask, as a church community, Where are we collectively being called to see where Christ is present in our world and recognize our alignment with Christ comes as we allow the Spirit to draw us into the points of greatest need within our neighborhoods, our cities, and our world? And then, individually, we can each ask, Where am I being called to be the Good Samaritan—to respond to a need that has arisen "on the way"? I am never so busy that I do not have margin in my schedule to lend a helping hand, so where and in what ways am I called to be present to, advocating for, or tangible to assisting those in need as a regular part of the weekly routines of my life?

THE BLESSING FOR THOSE WHO GIVE

The apostle Paul was a fundraiser. It was an essential part of his own calling to secure financial contributions for two things: for the poor and to support his anticipated ministry through Rome and onward to Spain. He turned to those who had the means on the assumption that their giving was a vital means by which they would engage their world and participate in what God was doing. And, not to be missed, he viewed this as vital to their own faith; it was and is now a vital spiritual practice: a means by which we see and participate in what God is doing in our communities and in our world.

The apostle thus urges his readers to not give reluctantly or out of a sense of obligation or "under compulsion" but with good cheer (2 Cor 9:7)—an alacrity reflecting an appreciation for the generosity, the abundance, of God. And what they will come to experience, quite simply, is that in their giving, they themselves are enriched (2 Cor 9:11).

Many of us who have a ministry of fundraising appreciate the insights offered through a little book—almost a booklet—by Henri Nouwen, *The Spirituality of Fund Raising*. Nouwen speaks of this as a ministry wherein we invite others to invest their financial resources where they are needed as a means of leveraging those resources for the kingdom of God. And he speaks of this as a ministry not only for the opportunity to make such an investment but also because in giving we let go of a false security or crutch: the illusion of financial security.[8] He observes that money touches us deeply and in giving it away, we are freed from trusting in our wealth or riches and can move toward a greater appreciation of where true security is found.

But we can go further. As noted, the ministry of fundraising is a way by which we invite others to see what God is doing. The apostle Paul raised funds for both the poor in Jerusalem and for his ministry to Spain and, in so doing, highlighted the actions and initiative of the Spirit and invited participation in this work. As such, this spiritual practice—the giving of our financial means—is a vital way by which we let go of false security *and* invest in the lives and ministries of others; it is a win-win. We can welcome those who invite us to give, to invest, because they help us see that which has the potential to capture our imagination: investing in an orphanage, low-cost housing for the homeless, education or religious outreach. Those who do the fundraising tell a story and invite us to give. We can say no, and genuine fundraisers will respect this. We do not give under compulsion, but with a generosity of heart that brings us into something—a cause or a ministry—that does not build our own lives or our own kingdoms, but rather the kingdom of God. We give to the one-time investment in a project; and we learn to give as a regular practice of contributing to a cause or ministry.

INTERCESSORY PRAYER

As with financial giving, intercessory prayer is also a practice of engagement, and it can also be considered more briefly than hospitality and works of mercy. Naturally, we pray for ourselves—our work, our health, our needs, and the needs of those who are near and dear to us, including family, friends, and colleagues. Similarly, a church community will surely pray that God would bless the ministry of their particular church. But when we speak of practices of engagement, we are thinking of the prayers of the people of God that are not specifically about themselves and their own needs. It is the ministry of prayer that is offered quietly and consistently, as a means of participation in the high priestly prayers of the risen and ascended Christ.

Christ is our high priest; he is ever interceding for the church and for the world. And when we pray for the church and for the world; for the needs of our cities, our neighborhoods, and civic leaders; and for the schools, universities, hospitals, social agencies, businesses, and sister churches in our cities, we are praying with Christ. Ideally, this is a regular practice: we are not merely praying for ourselves, but for others—other churches, other businesses, other schools, as well as our neighbors. We read the morning news not as a matter of mere interest or curiosity, but as a way to inform our prayers: a problem or crisis on the other side of the world leads us to pray. We read the news attentive to how we can pray with our high priest.

Each of these practices can have a collective expression, perhaps as a church community. Together we offer hospitality. Together we can ask how we are being called to be an instrument of works of mercy. Together we can ask how a portion of our annual budget can be invested strategically, not merely to build up our church but as an act of generosity and participation in what God is doing in the world. And together we, week in and week out, in the prayers of the people, bring our lament as we feel the pain of the world and make our case that God would graciously intervene and show grace and mercy in a time of need.

The example of the church community then provides a model for each individual and family to, in like manner, come to see these practices of engagement as a vital means by which we decenter our lives—meaning we increasingly come to see that however important our own work and vocation is, we are not the center of the universe; it is not all about us. We learn this. However, one more thing needs to be **HOWEVER IMPORTANT OUR OWN WORK AND VOCATION IS, WE ARE NOT THE CENTER OF THE UNIVERSE; IT IS NOT ALL ABOUT US.** said, by way of conclusion: the need for quiet—perhaps even that our generosity and engagement with the world would be marked by anonymity and secrecy. Jesus stresses we do not do these works of piety or spiritual engagement as a way to bring attention to ourselves (Mt 6:1-6). Rather, he calls us to learn the value of letting the focus be elsewhere. We do not trumpet our giving (Mt 6:2); we do not make a point of letting everyone know that we are praying for them or for the world. We learn the value of the under-stated; we do it because it is the right thing to do and we need no credit, no affirmation, no praise. We can learn to avoid the need to let the world know through a social media account what it is we have done or are doing. And the point Jesus makes is that this disposition or attitude is essential if we are to know the spiritual benefits of these very practices—if we are to know the grace that comes through practices of engagement, the grace of seeing God in all things. Further, in an age of distraction, when social media can so easily insulate us from the needs of the world, these practices foster our capacity to be more fully present to our world and to what God is doing in our world.

QUESTIONS FOR REFLECTION AND DISCUSSION

1. In reading through the four practices of engagement, which one stood out to you as a practice you might give more attention to—that is, incorporate more fully into your life?

2. Where have you known the grace of God—the blessing of God—experienced when you offered hospitality, or en-gaged in a work of mercy, or gave of your means, or sup-ported an effort or cause through intercessor prayer?

9

SUSTAINING A
RESILIENT HOPE

WE DO OUR WORK and fulfill our vocations in a discouraging world. There is no avoiding this. For one and all—regardless of calling or vocation—we will face one set back after another. Things will not unfold smoothly and easily, not for anyone. And thus, those who do good work and fulfill their calling or purpose will be those who sustain a hopeful realism. We can only truly be present to the here and now, to the situation as it actually is, and contribute something of lasting value if we engage our circumstances with some measure of hope.

Further, within the organizations, churches, and businesses of which we are a part, our calling—the work that is our responsibility—will always include to some degree the need for us to be a source of renewed hope for others. And this means that we are agents of encouragement within our homes, our places of work and worship, and in our communities. This being the case, it is essential that we have a clear understanding of what it means to be a person of hope and, further, what we can learn about how to foster communities and centers of hopeful realism. Thinking this way means we appreciate a number of things.

First, and fundamentally, hope and encouragement are always offered against the backdrop of realism—naming reality, however dark or difficult or depressing. In a June 2020 article in the Canadian journal for higher education *University Affairs*, Jessica Riddell makes the helpful distinction between what she calls "toxic positivity" and "critical hope."[1] By toxic positivity she means something that I fear plagues so many religious communities: pseudo assurances that everything will be fine; that "God is in control"; that if we just hang in there and get along, all will work itself out fine. She actually speaks of toxic positivity as a power structure, a social system that in effect does not allow for disagreement or discontent or uncomfortable conversations. And, I would add, does not allow for anger.

Speaking hope is not about maudlin assurances. It is not about feel-good false comfort. Rather, it is about speaking to the possibilities of grace very specifically against and within the darkness and fragmentation of our lives and our work. And this means we need to be able to speak of the darkness, and rage against the night. A parent can only encourage a child if and as they have heard all about the bully or the deep shame of walking home from school with what they feel is an unfair report card. We can only encourage and bring hope if and as we feel the pain of someone else's loss, learning the grace of "mourning with those who mourn." And we can only live in hope if and as we learn what it means to lament: to feel the full force of our own losses or setbacks.

For example, church communities that are vital centers of a resilient hope are not those that only sing happy songs and default to inspirational stories as the "sermon" for that Sunday. Rather, they are congregations that know how to name and feel the pain of the world and the pain of their members; it is this posture of lament that is the necessary backdrop to renewed hope.

Second, hope and encouragement are about the refusal to accept this reality as the status quo. Hope is the antithesis of resignation and fatalism. We recognize reality, but women and men of hope have an insistence about them—or better, a *persistence*. They do not give up. In the language of the book of Romans, in the midst of trial or difficulty, they *persevere*. That text from Paul assures readers that if they persevere, hope does not disappoint (Rom 5:3-5). They consistently focus on what can be done rather than despairing about what cannot be done. And often they persist in the face of what might seem like hopeless circumstances. They are not naive to the situation; but they persevere in their vision for the good, the noble, and the excellent. This usually means something as simple as the life principle that we take one step at a time; we just do what needs to be done now, today, recognizing that sometimes that is all we can do: take one step.

However, in speaking to what it means to persevere, we need to add an important qualifier. Those marked by hope are also those whose lives and work and relationships are marked by honor, integrity, and virtue. They persevere with a parallel commitment to doing the right thing the right way. A vivid way to illustrate this is through the contrast between nonviolent peaceful protest and violent acts that attempt to resolve an issue through force. Perseverance and persistence and doggedness and determination are all profound indicators of hope; but violence is a sign that we have actually given up—we are hopeless. Few people exemplified this as powerfully as John Lewis—the American congressional leader from Georgia—famous, in part, for his walk across the bridge named after a Ku Klux Klan leader. Lewis refused to act as he had been acted on—with violence; he refused to resort to violence to achieve political gains.

In the course of our daily lives and work, this means a carpenter refuses to be compromised in the quality of the work being done, that a surgeon will cut no corners, that a professor will come to a lecture having done due diligence, that an athlete will not take performance enhancing substances, that those in leadership will work within and honor the system of governance even if it means they get outvoted. Athletes will not cheat; they will honor the rules of the game. Business entrepreneurs will not game the system or violate their commitment to doing business in a way that honors their suppliers and their clients. Administrators will not manipulate but work openly—with transparency and accountability—with their colleagues. Politicians will uphold the law and work within the system of governance—honoring it—to achieve their desired outcomes. So yes, hope is about perseverance and persistence, but only if and as it means a commitment to working with courage and patience in a manner that reflects honor, virtue, and character.

Third, those who are hopeful are also those who are meek. By this I mean quite simply something along the lines of the biblical understanding of meekness: that if we are hopeful, we do not carry resentments. We let the wrongs of the past be in the past, and we are willing to work with those who may well have wronged us and offended us and let us down. We get beyond vengeance.

> **HOPE IS ABOUT PERSEVERANCE AND PERSISTENCE, BUT ONLY IF AND AS IT MEANS A COMMITMENT TO WORKING WITH COURAGE AND PATIENCE IN A MANNER THAT REFLECTS HONOR, VIRTUE, AND CHARACTER.**

Without doubt, our journey in the work we do—in the fulfillment of our vocations—will include one or more, if not multiple times, when others will do something that impedes our work, goes against us, undermines us, sets us back. We will be treated unjustly and dishonorably. This will happen. And these people will not just go away. The problem is that it is relatively easy to live perpetually with the resentment. But it gains little.

I am not for a moment suggesting we deny the wrong that has been done. At some point, however, we move on and realize that in the workplace—where we may well have been wronged—we name the reality of the wrong and then we set it aside; we refuse to carry the wrong as a perpetual burden or obstacle to our capacity to work with this person.

Are there limits to what I have just suggested? Can someone work closely with another, a person who has in the past been their abuser? Yes, there are limits. But I have been impressed with the grace of those who have been deeply wronged and yet found in themselves the capacity to dig deep and find the inner strength to seek the greater good and not let their own resentments and wounds undermine their capacity to do the work to which they have been called.

What comes to mind are the words of the apostle Paul, notably in his letters to the Corinthians: his refusal to pay back wrong for wrong but a resolve to give himself to, as he puts it, "purity, knowledge, patience, kindness, holiness of spirit, genuine love, truthful speech," even if they are "treated as impostors" (2 Cor 6:6-8).

Fourth, we need to consider a danger that emerges when we are discouraged—for whatever reason. We live and work in a discouraging world; in our work, regardless of our vocations, we will have multiple points of setback. If we believe in what we are doing, and are working toward something of value and worth, we will get discouraged. Getting discouraged is not in itself a problem. When someone says they never get discouraged, I wonder either where they live—must be nice—or, I realize they are not really working toward something that truly matters. If you are working toward something of worth and value, there will be setbacks. You will get discouraged. The question, really, is this: Will this discouragement settle in? Will it take root? If discouragement is allowed to settle—to get into our bones and bloodstream—we are no longer merely discouraged: we are cynics. The cynic is someone who lives perpetually from a disposition that is useless, and more, it is toxic. It makes the situation worse. Thus, while being discouraged is not in itself a problem—it actually may be a sign you are doing something that matters and is therefore worth doing—we cannot allow discouragement to settle, to set up camp in our hearts. Hope is an imperative for any good work we might be called to do—in the arts, education, business, or in civic or religious leadership. We need to not only encourage one another but also be able to *be* encouraged—always able and tenderhearted enough to have our hope renewed.

It might be a hike in the foothills with a spouse, an evening with good food and conversation with friends, working on a project with a granddaughter, an early morning birding expedition, or meeting up with a friend midmorning or midafternoon with an appropriate beverage in hand. Or, without doubt, as significant as anything, the Christian liturgy—the common worship and prayers of God's people: the ancient hymns sung, the creed recited, the Scriptures read and proclaimed, the Psalms said and read and sung, and, most of all, the Eucharist—the gathering of God's people at the Communion Table.

> **WE NEED TO NOT ONLY ENCOURAGE ONE ANOTHER BUT ALSO BE ABLE TO *BE* ENCOURAGED— ALWAYS ABLE AND TENDERHEARTED ENOUGH TO HAVE OUR HOPE RENEWED.**

The point is that lest we fall into a cynical state of mind, we need to be encouraged. We do not need pseudo encouragement; we do not need flattery or platitudes. We do not need premature assurances that God is in control when all the evidence around us is to the contrary. And yet, what we know is that even though pseudo encouragement is empty and of no help, we do need to be in the company of those who know what it means to move from discouragement to renewed hope.

Fifth, hope is about creativity and innovation—in the context of what is actually the case, not what we wish was and is the case—to see what good, what constructive outcome, what possibilities can emerge from this situation. There is an image that has over the years captured this so very effectively for me.

A number of years ago, my wife, Joella, and I were in Toronto, Canada, having lunch with our friends Doug and Judy Wiebe. As we were ordering our meal, Joella commented on the dishes the restaurant was using, which were particularly unique and beautiful. Then, a few minutes later we heard a crash coming from the kitchen area—and assumed it was one of these dishes. Joella's response was, "Pity those fragments will be thrown into the garbage . . . because they would actually make a great mosaic."

Doug immediately jumped up and left our table. Two minutes later, he was back proudly raising up a cheap plastic bag holding the shards from the broken dish. Doug and Judy moved to Winnipeg to provide pastoral leadership for the Exchange, a congregation in the heart of the rougher part of the city. I visited them during their first year and dropped by—midweek—to see the venue where the Exchange met. They were keen to show me the space but also something else: the mosaics—twenty or twenty-five of them—done by women who came off the streets of Winnipeg. Broken lives; broken bodies. They came once a week to the Exchange to work on their mosaics—not working from mass produced fine tesserae tiles but with broken glass and pottery pieces: bringing beauty out of that which was broken. And, it goes without saying, coming perhaps to see the possibility of beauty and healing in their own lives.

When we speak this way—about good that comes from a situation—this is not for a moment because we are minimizing the wrong, the abuse, even perhaps a tragedy. It is not about downplaying the fragmentation of our situation with platitudes about "there is a reason for everything" or any other form of false comfort. But we can still speak of how good and beauty and transformation can come out of deep pain and loss and fragmentation—as captured by the image of the mosaic from the broken shards.

Women and men of hope have a fundamental capacity to innovate, adapt, and adjust their plans and priorities and vision in response to the new reality in which they find themselves—even when, if not *particularly* when, their circumstances seem so very challenging and difficult. Rather than despair, they consider what might be possible in the situation. They are entrepreneurial if they are in business. They shift to alternate forms of classroom instruction if they are teachers during a pandemic. Whatever their vocation, they have a resilience that is evident in being adaptive—thinking of what is and might be possible in this time and in this place. Rather than bemoaning what was or what might have been, they give their mental and emotional energy into what perhaps could be.

This is why the arts are so vitally important in our lives. They do two things simultaneously—at least two: they comfort and they encourage. I think of the tremendous opportunity my wife and I had to be present a few years ago for the Calgary Philharmonic Chorus rendition of Rachmaninoff's *Vespers*. Oh yes, the Russians know how to lament; they are masters of drawing us into a deep awareness of the human condition. But I come away not feeling sorry for myself or despair for the world, but ever hopeful, ever more encouraged to be what I am called to be and contribute what I am invited to contribute in the investment of my time and energy.

But more, the arts also foster within all of us the capacity for innovation—possibility thinking. In business, in education and science and social work, and in pastoral leadership, we need to tend to our artists: musicians, poets, painters, sculptors, actors. Whether in the concert hall or the theater stage, whether in the context of Christian liturgy or when we gather around the piano in our homes, those in the arts play a vital role in sustaining the hope of a community or a nation.

We need to stress, though, that the genius of the arts is not that they paper over our pain and loss; it is actually a pseudo form of art—perhaps mere sentimentality or kitsch—that does not speak hope very specifically into our dark circumstances. This perspective is brilliantly present to us in the Japanese art form known as *kintsugi*, which means "golden" links, or is also spoken of as golden repair. It is the art of repairing a piece of broken pottery in a way that does not try to hide the breakage but actually treats it as part of the history of this particular object. The crack is actually inlaid with gold—thus in effect highlighting and bringing a unique beauty out of the crack. And from a life perspective, it is a way of thinking—and action, in a way—that brings beauty and transformation out of wrong. Again, nothing in the arts suggests that wrong is not wrong. It is rather that we do not despair but look and see what good, what beauty, what innovation might present itself. And the artists in our midst cultivate this capacity for all of us, regardless of our specific callings.

And then, finally, we need to speak of patience—patience with God and thus patience with our circumstances, patience with ourselves, and with others. Theologians speak of hope as eschatological: we live now in light of what we know is coming—a confidence we have that one day, God will make all things well. This is not—and this must be stressed— a means of escaping the present or disregarding the wrongs or challenges of the current situation. Not at all. It is merely and rather that we are fully present to our present with a confidence of what is yet to come. And thus, we are present to the current situation as women and men of patience.

Our confidence, our hope, is not ultimately in our own work, but in the work of God. Our hope lies there, rests there, is focused there—on the grace and power and purpose of the living and ascended Christ. And we are thus patient, letting God do God's work in God's time. The genius of this perspective is the assumption that we have not given up on God and that hope is ultimately about saying, with Dame Julian, "all shall be well, and all shall be well and all manner of things shall be well." The arts and our mutual encouragement keep us anchored in this long-term vision for the God who will make all things well. And as such, patience is a fundamental mark of what it means to be a people of hope.

Now it is important to stress that the above elements or dimensions of hope are of a whole. Thus, we lament, but we do not despair. We get discouraged, but we guard our hearts lest we become cynics. We are patient, but our patience is not fatalism but rather a quiet resolve evident in our persistence. And without doubt, we can only hold all of this together if we are connected to and part of institutions and communities that sustain together a hopeful resilience. No one can sustain a vibrant hope in isolation from vital and hopeful communities and organizations. And thus to stress, it is imperative and essential that churches, schools, universities, and businesses—especially smaller, owner-operated businesses, including restaurants, coffee shops, grocery stories, and neighborhood hardware stores—see themselves as beacons of hope within their communities.

What this assumes, of course, is that we know what it means for us, as individuals, to live with a resilient hope, and that this is part of what we bring to our homes, our workplaces, our church communities, and our neighborhoods. We hear and live the words of Galatians 6:9 that we do not grow weary in doing well.

QUESTIONS FOR REFLECTION AND DISCUSSION

1. Where and in what ways are you experiencing discouragement, disappointment, and a heaviness of heart?

2. What for you is a source of encouragement—precisely in the face of where you are feeling what you spoke of in response to the previous question?

CONCLUSION

WHEN ALL IS SAID AND DONE, two things need to be stressed—as a final word. And they need to be said *together*. The two are beautifully found and expressed in the experience of Mary at the annunciation in her response to the angel Gabriel and then immediately after as she makes her way to a visit in the hill country with her cousin Elizabeth: she accepts the call of God; she receives the encouragement of her cousin.

In the encounter with Gabriel her response says it all: "Here I am, a servant of the Lord." Or, as it is expressed in a contemporary sung version within many Christian communities, simply and powerfully: "Here I am, Lord." It was Mary's call and choice, as wonderfully captured by the poem by W. H. Auden, who puts this into the words of Gabriel to say:

> What I am willed to ask, your own
> Will has to answer; child it lies
> Within your power of choosing to
> Conceive the Child who chooses you.[1]

God chooses us; God calls us. To the here and now. And here, Auden captures the wonder of the moment: that God chooses us and calls us, but now it behooves us to accept and

> **GOD CHOOSES US AND CALLS US, BUT NOW IT BEHOOVES US TO ACCEPT AND EMBRACE THIS CALL.**

embrace this call, to take personal responsibility for our lives. Discerning vocation is something that falls to each one—each person before God recognizing and responding to the call of God. No one can do this for you; it is you, before God, invited to be a steward of this life, your life.

And then we read that Mary went to visit Elizabeth, and there received the blessing of the older woman—confirming the call of Mary. This is a reminder that in our lives and in our work, we are not alone, and we cannot do this—discern and embrace our vocation—if we are alone. Yes, we need to have the courage and grace to take responsibility for our own lives; but we cannot do this until and unless we are connected—in community, in relationship, in accountability even to others.

Every chapter in this reflection on *Your Calling Here and Now* makes this twofold assumption. First, we need to take personal responsibility for our lives. And, of equal importance, we need to be in conversation with and accountable to others. Whether it is in recognizing and accepting our circumstances, or whether it comes to seeing ourselves in truth. Actually, each chapter in this reflection on the stewardship of our lives assumes we take personal responsibility but that we do so in conversation and accountability. And in the end, in speaking about hope, we cannot sustain hope in isolation from others. We need their timely words; we need others on the journey with us. Thus, if there is an abiding message in all of this, it is surely that we cultivate these connections and these conversations; we do not attempt to navigate this life and this road on our own. We need to be alert to those who might want to control or presume to play a parental role in our lives, of course. But we get to know who we can lean on and depend on—who will be a source of counsel and encouragement. The contributions of those who are genuinely coming alongside and not presuming to be "god" to us—they are co-discerners, mutual encouragers, companions on the way. When we find them, we have found gold. Nurture those connections; lean into them in a time of decision, transition, or discouragement. They are to us a means of grace.

> **WE CANNOT SUSTAIN HOPE IN ISOLATION FROM OTHERS.**

NOTES

1. AT THIS TIME AND IN THIS PLACE

[1]I am borrowing this phrase from the title of a book, *At This Time and in This Place: Vocation and Higher Education*, ed. David S. Cunningham (Oxford: Oxford University Press, 2016).

[2]Gethsemane is a reference to Jesus' encounter with the Father prior to his arrest and trial; Gabriel is the angel that met Mary and advised her of the invitation to be the God-bearer; the burning bush is a reference to Moses in the desert and his encounter with God, who called him to lead the people of Israel out of slavery.

2. THE STEWARDSHIP OF OUR LIVES

[1]Fyodor Dostoevsky, *The Brothers Karamazov: A Novel in Four Parts with Epilogue*, trans. Richard Pevear and Larissa Volokhonsky (New York: Farrar, Straus and Giroux, 1990), 44.

[2]Eugene H. Peterson, *Under the Unpredictable Plant: An Exploration in Vocational Holiness* (Grand Rapids, MI: Eerdmans, 1994), 21-22.

3. CALLING AND CALLINGS

[1]Bonnie J. Miller-McLemore, *Also a Mother: Work and Family as Theological Dilemma* (Nashville: Abingdon Press, 1994).

[2]I am grateful to Father Thomas Ryan for suggesting this way of thinking about multiple obligations—the image of concentric circles.

[3]L. Gregory Jones, "Negotiating the Tensions of Vocation," *The Scope of Our Art: The Vocation of the Theological Teacher*, ed. L. Gregory Jones and Stephanie Paulsell (Grand Rapids, MI: Eerdmans, 2002), 209.

[4]Shaun C. Henson and Michael J. Lakey, eds., *Academic Vocation in the Church and Academy Today: 'And With All Of Your Mind'* (Aldershot, Hampshire, United Kingdom: Ashgate Publishing, 2016).

[5]Mary Catherine Bateson, *Composing a Life* (New York: Penguin, 1989), 233-35.

4. CAREER TRANSITIONS

[1]Nell Irvin Painter, *Old in Art School: A Memoir of Starting Over* (Berkeley, CA: Counterpoint, 2018).

5. TENDING TO THE LIFE OF THE MIND

[1]Gordon T. Smith, "The University Mission: Cultivating the Life of the Mind," *Thinking Christianly* blog, February 1, 2021, www.ambrose.edu/thinkingchristianly.
[2]Gerard W. Hughes, *God of Surprises*, 3rd ed. (Grand Rapids, MI: Eerdmans, 2008), 17.
[3]Harry Blamires, *The Christian Mind* (New York: Seabury Press, 1963), 42-60.
[4]Gordon T. Smith, "Cultivating the Life of the Mind: Threat No. 1—Pragmatism," *Thinking Christianly* blog, April 15, 2021, www.ambrose.edu/thinkingchristianly.
[5]Martha C. Nussbaum, *Not for Profit: Why Democracy Needs the Humanities* (Princeton, NJ: Princeton University Press, 2010).
[6]Gordon T. Smith, "Cultivating the Life of the Mind: Threat No. 1—Sentimentalism," *Thinking Christianly* blog, May 1, 2021, www.ambrose.edu/thinkingchristianly.
[7]Gordon T. Smith, "Cultivating the Life of the Mind: Threat No. 3, Partisan Propaganda," *Thinking Christianly* blog, May 15, 2021, www.ambrose.edu/thinkingchristianly.
[8]*St. Athanasius on the Incarnation*, rev ed., trans. and edited by a religious of the CSMV (Oxford, England: A. R. Mowbray, 1953), 3-4.
[9]A. W. Tozer, *The Christian Book of Mystical Verse: A Collection of Poems, Hymns, and Prayers for Devotional Reading* (Harrisburg, PA: Christian Publications, 1963).
[10]For a good discussion of the merits of digital versus hard copy reading, see Maryanne Wolf, *Reader Come Home: The Reading Brain in a Digital World* (New York: HarperCollins, 2018).
[11]For an excellent guide to reading, see Karen Swallow Prior, *On Reading Well: Finding the Good Life Through Reading Great Books* (Grand Rapids, MI: Brazos, 2018).

6. THE WORK OF OUR HANDS

[1]Matthew B. Crawford, *Shop Class as Soulcraft: An Inquiry into the Value of Work* (New York: Penguin Random House, 2009), 23.
[2]*The Rule of St. Benedict*, trans. Anthony C. Meisel and M. L. del Mastro (New York: Doubleday, 1975), 86.
[3]Ole Thorstensen, *Making Things Right: The Simple Philosophy of a Working Life*, trans. Sean Kinsella (New York: Penguin Random House, 2017), 41.
[4]Thorstensen, *Making Things Right*, 91.
[5]Brother Lawrence, *The Practice of the Presence of God*, https://d2y1pz2y630308.cloudfront.net/15471/documents/2016/10/Brother%20Lawrence-The%20Practice%20of%20the%20Presence%20of%20God.pdf.

7. VOCATIONAL THINKING MEANS ORGANIZATIONAL THINKING

[1]Gordon T. Smith, "Want to Change the World? Invest in Institutions," The Gospel Coalition, January 31, 2019, www.thegospelcoalition.org/article/change-world-institutions.

[2]Micah White, "Why Are Our Protests Failing?," www.micahmwhite.com/susan-cole-toronto.

[3]James K. A. Smith, *Imagining the Kingdom: How Worship Works* (Grand Rapids, MI: Baker Academic, 2013).

[4]Michael Jinkins and Deborah Bradshaw Jinkins, *The Character of Leadership: Political Realism and Public Virtue in Nonprofit Organizations* (San Francisco: Jossey-Bass Publishers, 1998), 62.

8. PRACTICES OF ENGAGEMENT

[1]Thomas Aquinas, *Summa Theologiae*, III, Q. 40, A. 1, Ad 2.

[2]Dietrich Bonhoeffer, *Life Together* and *Prayer Book of the Bible*, trans. Daniel W. Bloesch and James B. Burtness, Dietrich Bonhoeffer Works, vol. 5 (Philadelphia: Fortress Press, 1996), 74-75.

[3]*The Rule of St. Benedict*, trans. Anthony C. Meisel and M. L. del Mastro (New York: Doubleday, 1975).

[4]Henri J. M. Nouwen, *Reaching Out: The Three Movements of the Spiritual Life* (New York: Doubleday, 1975), 51.

[5]Nouwen, *Reaching Out*, 69.

[6]They debated if food sacrificed to idols could be consumed by Christians. And they debated if the Christian community needed to observe special feast days.

[7]John Wesley Sermon 16, "Means of Grace" in Albert C. Outler, ed. *The Works of John Wesley. Vol I. Sermons I, 1-33.* (Nashville: Abingdon Press, 1984), II. I., 381. 65.

[8]Henri Nouwen: *The Spirituality of Fund Raising* (Nashville: Upper Room Ministries, 2004), 14-15.

9. SUSTAINING A RESILIENT HOPE

[1]Jessica Riddell, "Combatting Toxic Positivity with Critical Hope," *University Affairs*, June 19, 2020, www.universityaffairs.ca/opinion/adventures-in-academe/combatting-toxic-positivity-with-critical-hope.

CONCLUSION

[1]W. H. Auden, *For the Time Being: A Christmas Oratorio*, ed. Alan Jacobs (Princeton, NJ: Princeton University Press, 2013; poem originally published in 1944), 16-17.